Harvard University Class of 1833

Memorials of the Class of 1833 of Harvard College

Harvard University Class of 1833

Memorials of the Class of 1833 of Harvard College

ISBN/EAN: 9783337178536

Printed in Europe, USA, Canada, Australia, Japan

Cover: Foto ©ninafisch / pixelio.de

More available books at **www.hansebooks.com**

MEMORIALS

OF

THE CLASS OF 1833

OF HARVARD COLLEGE

PREPARED FOR THE

𝔉𝔦𝔣𝔱𝔦𝔢𝔱𝔥 𝔄𝔫𝔫𝔦𝔳𝔢𝔯𝔰𝔞𝔯𝔶 𝔬𝔣 𝔱𝔥𝔢𝔦𝔯 𝔊𝔯𝔞𝔡𝔲𝔞𝔱𝔦𝔬𝔫

BY THE CLASS SECRETARY

WALDO HIGGINSON

CAMBRIDGE:
JOHN WILSON AND SON.
𝔘𝔫𝔦𝔳𝔢𝔯𝔰𝔦𝔱𝔶 𝔓𝔯𝔢𝔰𝔰.
1883.

PREFATORY NOTE.

THE CLASS BOOK and all records of the Class of 1833 were burnt in the great fire in Boston in 1872, when their custodian was in Europe.

This irreparable loss must necessarily diminish the value of the following pages, as it has certainly increased the labor of preparing them.

It is hoped, however, that the memorials, here submitted, of widely scattered classmates will give as much pleasure to the survivors, as their collection has to the Secretary.

WALDO HIGGINSON.

BOSTON, June 1, 1883.

TABLE OF CONTENTS.

PREFATORY NOTE	5
LIST OF GRADUATES OF 1833	9
NECROLOGY OF GRADUATES OF 1833	11
MEMOIRS OF THE DECEASED	17
NOTICES OF THE SURVIVORS	97
LIST OF STUDENTS, SOME TIME IN THE CLASS OF 1833, WHO DID NOT GRADUATE WITH IT	145
NOTICES OF STUDENTS MENTIONED ABOVE	147

GRADUATES

OF THE CLASS OF 1833.

*Allen, John Clarke	17
Andrews, Samuel Page	97
Baker, James Loring	100
*Bates, Charles Jarvis	27
*Bolton, Thomas	46
*Bourne, Thomas Rotch	21
Bowen, Francis	100
Clark, Luther	103
Crafts, George Inglis	104
Curtis, Hiram Keith	105
*Dehon, William	66
Dix, John Homer	106
Draper, Charles	107
*Eaton, George	78
Ellis, George Edward	109
*Foster, Andrew	84
Gay, Sydney Howard	112
*Gray, Henry Yancey	56
*Greenough, David Stoddard	77
*Harding, Fisher Ames	24
*Harrington, Joseph, Jr.	30
Hartshorn, Charles Warren	115
Higginson, Waldo	116
*Jackson, Charles	53
*Jarvis, William Porter	86

*Kelly, Moses	43
Livermore, Abiel Abbot	117
Lovering, Joseph	121
Lowell, Robert Traill Spence	128
*Lyman, John Chester	91
Mack, William	130
Nichols, George Henry	131
*Parker, Frederic	35
Peck, William Dandridge	132
*Peirce, Charles Henry	33
*Pendleton, Isaac Purnell	22
*Pope, Thomas Butler	37
*Porter, Huntington	19
Prichard, William Mackay	133
*Rutter, Josiah	75
Stearns, Edward Josiah	133
*Stone, John Osgood	71
*Torrey, Rufus Campbell	89
Torrey, Henry Warren	136
Tucker, Nathaniel Saville	137
Watson, Winslow Marston	138
*Webster, Fletcher	38
Welch, Charles Alfred	139
*Weld, Christopher Minot	82
*White, Joseph	20
*Whiting, William	57
*Whitney, Frederic Augustus	86
Wigglesworth, Thomas	141
Wyman, Morrill	141
*Wyman, Jeffries	60
*Young, Richard Sharpe	80

56

NECROLOGY.

JOHN CLARKE ALLEN.
Died at North Andover, Mass. . . . . . . June 24, 1834.

HUNTINGTON PORTER.
Died at Rainsford Island, Boston Harbor . . June 21, 1836.

JOSEPH WHITE.
Died at the McLean Asylum, Somerville, Mass. July 1, 1838.

THOMAS ROTCH BOURNE.
Died at Sandwich, Mass. . . . . Oct. 27, 1839.

ISAAC PURNELL PENDLETON.
Died at Caroline Co., Eastern Shore, Md. . . Sept. 1840.

FISHER AMES HARDING.
Died at Detroit, Mich. . . . . Aug. 4, 1846.

CHARLES JARVIS BATES.
Died at Salmadina, Gulf of Mexico . . . . Aug. 26, 1847.

JOSEPH HARRINGTON.
Died at San Francisco, Cal. . . . . Nov. 2, 1852.

CHARLES HENRY PEIRCE.
Died at Cambridge, Mass. . . . . June 16, 1855.

FREDERIC PARKER.
Died at Lowell, Mass. . . . . Jan. 29, 1857.

THOMAS BUTLER POPE.
Died at Roxbury, Mass. . . . . Jan. 15, 1862.

FLETCHER WEBSTER.
Killed at Second Battle of Bull Run, Prince William Co., Va. . . . . Aug. 30, 1862.

MOSES KELLY.
Died at Cleveland, O. . . . . Aug. 15, 1870.

THOMAS BOLTON.
Died at Cleveland, O. . . . . Feb. 1, 1871.

CHARLES JACKSON.
Died at Boston, Mass. . . . . July 30, 1871.

HENRY YANCEY GRAY.
Died at Charleston, S.C. . . . . July 4, 1872.

WILLIAM WHITING.
Died at Roxbury, Mass. . . . . June 29, 1873.

JEFFRIES WYMAN.
Died at Bethlehem, N.H. . . . . Sept. 4, 1874.

WILLIAM DEHON.
Died at Boston, Mass. . . . . May 20, 1875.

JOHN OSGOOD STONE.
Died at New York, N.Y. . . . . June 7, 1876.

JOSIAH RUTTER.
Died at Waltham, Mass. . . . . Sept. 3, 1876.

David Stoddard Greenough.
Died at Jamaica Plain, Mass. . . . . . . March 30, 1877.

George Eaton.
Died at Grantville, Mass. . . . . May 7, 1877.

Richard Sharpe Young.
Died at San Francisco, Cal. . . . . Aug. 9, 1877.

Christopher Minot Weld.
Died at Jamaica Plain, Mass. . . . . . . March 14, 1878.

Andrew Foster.
Died at Brooklyn, N.Y. . . . . Sept. 22, 1879.

William Porter Jarvis.
Died at Roxbury, Mass. . . . . May 29, 1880.

Frederic Augustus Whitney.
Died at Brighton, Mass. . . . . Oct. 21, 1880.

Rufus C. Torrey.
Died at Claiborne, Ala. . . . . Sept. 13, 1882.

John Chester Lyman.
Died at Doylestown, Pa. . . . . Feb. 27, 1883.

MEMOIRS OF THE DECEASED.

MEMOIRS OF THE DECEASED.

JOHN CLARKE ALLEN.[1]

JOHN CLARKE ALLEN was the son of Rev. Wilkes (H. C. 1801) and Mary (Morrill) Allen, and was born in Chelmsford, Mass., November 15, 1812. His father was for a long time minister in that town, and occupied a prominent place among the clergy of that part of the State. His mother was the daughter of Mr. James Morrill, for forty years deacon of the First Church in Boston, and a respected and successful merchant in that city. He was fitted for college in his native village, principally at the academy, then under the charge of Cranmore Wallace. During his college life, he evinced a very genial and social temper. In his autobiography in the Class Book, he speaks of himself as having been chiefly interested, when a boy, in books on medicine. In college he early formed the intention of being a physician, and his family represent him as resolved to devote himself to surgery.

From a near relative the Secretary has the following account of his last sickness: — "His early death was occasioned by a sprain of one ankle a few months before graduation. With his class, however, he received his degree; but this effort

[1] This memoir, and that of all those who died before 1858, were prepared for the "silver wedding" of the class in that year. They are here reprinted without material alterations.

increased his lameness, and proved to be his last appearance in public. The injury to the ankle soon induced a development of scrofula, which ended his days. After passing a few months at his father's house, then in Cambridge, under the care of the best surgeons of this vicinity, he went to the Massachusetts General Hospital, where he spent the winter of 1833-34; from the hospital, in March, he went to the South, and spent three months in Charleston, S. C., in the hope that change of air might benefit his disease. But in spite of this change, and the assiduous care of friends, the disease went on increasing in severity. In May he returned to his father's house, then in North Andover, and there cheerfully gave up all idea of recovery and of accomplishing his plan of life, laughing at pain, patiently enduring suffering, expressing his firm belief in the Christian religion, and embracing its comforts and hopes. He was gradually cut off from the outward world, by the loss of hearing and sight, and at last, on June 24, 1834, he died."

At a meeting of the class, held on the succeeding commencement, on motion of Mr. Fletcher Webster, it was

"*Voted*, That suitable notice be taken of the lamented death of our late classmate, John C. Allen; and that a committee of one be appointed for this purpose, to address a letter to the parents of the deceased, expressive of our esteem for our late associate, and of our sorrow at his untimely end."

Mr. E. J. Stearns was appointed on this committee. It is understood that the duty assigned him was duly performed, and that he received a suitable acknowledgment.

HUNTINGTON PORTER.

HUNTINGTON PORTER was the son of the Rev. Huntington (H. C. 1777) and Sarah (Moulton) Porter, and was born in Rye, N. H., December 4, 1812, where his father was minister. His mother was the daughter of General Jonathan Moulton, of Hampton, N. H. He was a nephew of the Rev. Eliphalet Porter (H. C. 1777), for a long time minister of the First Church in Roxbury, and a member of the Corporation of Harvard College from 1818 to 1833. He went to school in the academy at Greenland, N. H., and was fitted for college at Exeter.

After leaving college he went to his home in Rye, N. H., and spent the next winter in fitting two younger brothers for college. In May, 1834, he left home to seek occupation as a teacher, and was employed in that capacity successively in Philadelphia, in Pittsburg, and in Lexington, Ky. Soon after going to the last-named place, in the spring of 1835, he began the study of medicine at the medical school connected with the Transylvania University. During his residence in Lexington he joined the Presbyterian Church in that place. After staying there a year, in the latter part of May, 1836, he returned to New England, to visit his family and friends. A few days after his arrival he was taken sick with small-pox, to which he had been exposed on his journey. He was removed to the small-pox hospital on Rainsford Island, Boston Harbor, and died there June 21, 1836. His remains were deposited in the burial-ground of the island.

At the class meeting, on the subsequent commencement, it was

"*Voted*, That some notice of the recent demise of a classmate, Huntington Porter, is right and proper, and that a committee of one be appointed to address the father of the deceased in a manner expressive of the esteem of the class for their late friend, and of their sympathy with his bereaved relatives."

Waldo Higginson was appointed on this committee; and in accordance with this vote wrote to the Rev. Huntington Porter, at Rye, N. H., and received from him a reply which contains the following: — " It was my privilege to be with my son a considerable part of his very distressing sickness; and it was surprising to me to notice the patience, fortitude, composure, and resignation he manifested under it; and it was to me no small support to witness the evidence given in this and other ways, of his being prepared for the solemn event he saw before him."

JOSEPH WHITE.

JOSEPH WHITE was the son of Stephen and Harriet (Story) White, and was born at Salem, January 24, 1814. His mother was a sister of Judge Story. He was prepared for college chiefly at the Round Hill School, Northampton. After leaving college, he studied no profession, but assisted his father, who was engaged in lumbering on Grand Island in the St. Lawrence, where he owned valuable tracts, and in ship-building at East Boston.

He died at the McLean Asylum, in Somerville, on the morning of July 1, 1838.

THOMAS ROTCH BOURNE.

THOMAS ROTCH BOURNE was the son of Melatiah and Mary (Fearing) Bourne, and was born at Sandwich, Mass., January 6, 1811. His mother was the daughter of Brigadier-General Israel Fearing, a major in the Revolutionary War. He was fitted for college at the Sandwich Academy. At Cambridge he was modest, retiring, and reserved, although he filled with credit the post of President of the "Med. Fac." In person he was thought a model of manly beauty. He died at Sandwich, October 27, 1839. A notice of his career and character, written by Mr. Thomas B. Pope, appeared in the Boston Daily Advertiser a few days after his death, from which the following is extracted.

"Mr. Bourne shortly after graduating commenced the study of the law, and having spent three years at the Law School in Cambridge, and in the offices of the Hon. H. Vanderpoel of New York and of the Hon. John Reed of Massachusetts, was, upon examination, admitted to practise in the courts of the latter State. Already had his zeal and industry as a student secured for him the esteem and respect of the gentlemen with whom his studies were prosecuted. With a just confidence in his powers, with the knowledge that a faithful apprenticeship in the profession of his choice gave him at least a fair chance of success, and buoyed up with a proud and manly spirit, he sought independence and a home in the West, and established himself at Mt. Clemens, Michigan, as a lawyer and editor of one of the journals of Macomb County. He was prospering in his profession, was winning his way to the favor of his new townsmen, and already had their elective voice placed him in public stations of honorable advancement. When, little more than a year after he was first numbered among them, fever and ague seized upon him, his frame became prostrated, and he fell a victim to rapid pulmonary consumption. Having returned to the home of his father, during the past summer, in high hopes of recovering his health, it soon became apparent to his friends that the insidious disease was rapidly doing the work of destruction; and as the season slipped onward, they foresaw his dissolution could not long be deferred. For several weeks he had himself been aware that his way was plain, and led rapidly to the grave. Calmly and tranquilly resigned in his sufferings, and in the Christian hope of a happy hereafter, he sunk into death."

ISAAC PURNELL PENDLETON.

ISAAC PURNELL PENDLETON was the son of Edmund and Serena (Purnell) Pendleton, and was born in the city of Baltimore, on the 16th of August, 1813. Shortly after his birth, his parents removed to the Eastern Shore of Maryland, where his father died when he was ten years old. He was then placed in the family of his uncle, Philip C. Pendleton, where he lived till he came to Cambridge, in 1829. During the last half of the freshman year he was rusticated by the Faculty, and spent that time in the family of Rev. Mr. Ripley at Waltham, where he enjoyed the society and instruction of Mrs. Ripley, whom so many, and none more than he, have greatly venerated. He also passed the first half of the senior year at his home in Maryland. He was the handsome man of the class, and was naturally selected as the captain of the Harvard Washington Corps,— the duties of which office he performed with dignity and grace, not unbecoming the successor of Robert C. Winthrop, and the predecessor of Governor Williams of Maine. Though taking no rank as a scholar, he yet gave evidence of respectable abilities and a character which had much that was attractive and interesting. After leaving college, he resided with his aunt, Miss Purnell, in Caroline County, Eastern Shore of Maryland. Afterwards he spent some years in Martinsburg and in Winchester, Va. He returned to his aunt's residence in 1840, and died there of congestive fever in September of that year.

A friend who knew him well at Cambridge, and subsequently, writes thus: —

"The incidents of his life after leaving college were hardly such as friends desire to record. He had quite a comfortable patrimony, which he squandered in dissipation, although he never was reduced to actual want. But it must be mentioned, that he seemed to have reformed a short time before his illness, and his friends entertained for him hopes that he might become a useful man.

"When under the influence of liquor, he seemed to have a wild ferocity of disposition; but when sober, he was a gentleman in his whole deportment, and showed great kindness of heart and many noble qualities. Indeed, he had a number of very warm friends, who did all they could to rescue him from the habits which tyrannized over him."

Hon. John Bozman Kerr (H. C. 1830), who was a neighbor of Pendleton in Maryland, has also written of the reformation spoken of above. It took place in the summer of 1840, on his return to his home on the Eastern Shore of Maryland. For some months during this season he was temperate and devoted to his books, and was preparing for practice as a lawyer, for which profession he had never completed his studies. But early in the autumn he was seized with fever, (to which his previous habits rendered him an easy victim,) and died at the age of twenty-seven.

FISHER AMES HARDING.

FISHER AMES HARDING was the son of John and Julia (Battelle) Harding, and was born in Dover, Mass., January 23, 1811. His father was a farmer in that town. Having a great veneration for Fisher Ames, in whose household he had formerly lived for several years as a hired man, he named his son for that distinguished statesman. In the village school, Harding was soon distinguished as a boy of quick comprehension and great desire for knowledge; and he early indulged a longing for a collegiate education. After procuring his parents' consent to do all they could towards sending him to college, he sought the advice of Rev. Ralph Sanger (H. C. 1808), who was fortunately settled at the time over the church in Dover. By his advice and assistance, he was fitted for college, and joined the class at the beginning of the freshman year.

In college he was distinguished, not only for the observance of college rules, but also for scholarship, easily obtaining and keeping a rank within the first eight. He was respected and beloved by all, and passed through the four years with the reputation of being singularly guileless.

In his senior year he had the advantage of frequent intercourse with Daniel Webster, whose son was his room-mate. He had designed, after graduating, to keep school, until he should have provided means for studying his profession, which he resolved should be the law. But a short time before leaving college, Mr. Webster made the generous offer of taking him into his office as a law-student, and supporting him handsomely whilst there. This proposal, so honorable to Harding, was substantially accepted, though some of its liberality was modestly declined; and he spent the two years after graduating in Mr. Webster's office in Boston.

In 1835, he went to Chicago, and opened an office in connection with Henry Moore, Esq., who had also come from Massachusetts. In 1837, he removed to Detroit, and lived there during the rest of his life. He immediately formed a partnership with Mr. Fletcher Webster, which continued but a short time, in consequence of the latter's removal to Illinois. Afterwards he formed a connection with Mr. William Hale, now of Detroit, which continued till his own death.

In 1841 he was elected from his county to the State legislature. He had always taken an interest in public affairs, which was early instilled by his father's admiration of Fisher Ames and recollection of his conversation, and subsequently increased by his own intercourse with Daniel Webster. His sister writes: "Politics was the dream of his boyhood, and the engrossing subject that absorbed his after life." The conspicuous part he took in the proceedings of the Michigan House of Representatives attested that his early advantages had been wisely improved.

In 1841, also, he became associated with Mr. Morgan Bates in the editorship of the Detroit Daily Advertiser, then an able Whig journal, and he continued in this connection, except for about a year's interval, during the remainder of his life.

He was never married, and died of consumption, in Detroit, August 4, 1846, aged thirty-five.

In the columns of the Advertiser, of August 6, appeared the following: —

"DEATH OF MR. HARDING.

"It is our painful duty to announce the death of *Fisher Ames Harding*, Esq., one of the editors of this paper. He died at the residence of William Hale, Esq., of this city, on Tuesday evening at three o'clock. His health had been feeble for nearly two years, but did not assume an alarming character until within the past two weeks. The last week of his life was one of mental delirium, and of great apparent physical suffering."

Here follows a brief account of his life, which is the same as that given above.

"In the profession of the law, Mr. Harding was known as a thorough student and an upright counsellor, but his natural taste disqualified him for the turmoil and strife of professional life. He loved the shade of retiracy, and it was here, with the friends who saw him daily, that the dignity and purity of his character, the brilliancy of his talents, and the extent of his acquirements, commanded their admiration, while 'a daily beauty in his life' won their love and esteem. We dare not trust ourselves, under the feeling of the moment, to speak of our late friend and associate as we feel; we shall not exaggerate, however, when we say that his generous nature, his remarkable freedom from selfish feelings and conduct, and his native modesty, were acknowledged by, and won the respect of, even casual acquaintances. Though warmly attached to a political party, it disturbed not his social relations, and his political writings were not more distinguished by their purity and simplicity of style, than by their fairness and courtesy to his political opponents. He passed through the political agitations of the past few years an active participant, but we believe without incurring the personal animosity of any one, and he died without an enemy.

"To say that the death of such a man, of so much talent, of so much information, of so much goodness of heart, is a great loss to the community, would be to use a trite phrase to express a solemn feeling. To us personally, the loss of one from whom, after years of daily intercourse, we can recall not one instance of unkind or angry feeling or word, whose sound judgment, extensive knowledge, and social qualities we have had occasion daily to admire, is indeed irreparable. We may be permitted to grieve over his premature grave; for we feel

> ''T is manliness
> To be heart-broken here,
> For the grave of earth's best nobleness
> Is watered by a tear.'"

In the same paper, of August 6, appeared a call for a meeting of the members of the bar, at the United States Court-Room, and also for a meeting of the "Detroit Young Men's Society," at their rooms, to make arrangements for the funeral, which took place on that day from the house of Mr. Hale.

CHARLES JARVIS BATES.

CHARLES JARVIS BATES was the son of George and Elizabeth (Hall) Bates, and was born in Suffolk Place, Boston, November 24, 1813. His father took the degree of M. D. at Harvard College, 1813, but early relinquished practice. His mother was nearly connected with Governor Brooks and Judge Joseph Hall and Chief Justice Parker. She died in 1821. He went to a private school in Charlestown, kept by Mr. Gates, until in 1826 he entered the Boston Latin School, where he was fitted for college. He inherited from his mother a feeble constitution, was sickly as a boy, and his college studies were often interrupted by dyspepsia; nevertheless, he took a respectable rank as a scholar, and was exemplary in the performance of all his duties. His highest rank, however, was in the hearts of his classmates. He was not only generally beloved, but great confidence was felt in the firmness of his principles of truth and honor.

After leaving college he devoted himself immediately to the study of medicine, entering the office of Dr. William J. Walker, then living in Charlestown, in company with John O. Stone and Morrill Wyman. In 1836 he received the degree of M. D. He subsequently attended a course of medical lectures at the Pennsylvania University, Philadelphia, but did not take a degree. In March, 1838, he received permission to present himself before the Board of Naval Surgeons, and being successful was appointed Assistant Surgeon. On examination by another board, in May, 1845, he was promoted to the rank of Passed Assistant Surgeon, to date back to November, 1843, on account of absence from the country when others of his own standing had been promoted.

The following is taken from a letter of his to the class secretary, dated "U. S. Ship North Carolina, March 29, 1846": —

"My naval experiences have been considerable. I have been six and a half years at sea out of eight. Nearly three and a half I spent in the Mediterranean, and consider them to be the happiest of my life. I passed two years on the west coast of Africa, and these were perhaps the most unthankful of all. The rest of my sea life was on our own coast. I am much attached to the service; with all its *désagrémens*, there is much good in it. I prefer my associates to those of the shore; for I think I find more true friendship, — its candor, its warmth, its generosity, its feeling always undisguised. The navy officer has perhaps an advantage over the civilian in the choice of a friend, for he knows by reputation every other in the service, — the black mark always goes with its victim, and he can therefore choose with safety, or rather he can avoid with certainty."

At the time of his death the Rev. George E. Ellis was much with his father's family. In a letter dated Charlestown, August 29, 1848, he gives the following information about his life in the navy, and his death: —

"He used the opportunities which offered when on service in our ships, to travel in Italy and other countries. His interest in his profession was great, and he cultivated a taste for some of the departments of natural science. I have occasionally met with his companions in the public service, and with his acquaintances of the last few years; and a fortnight ago I met in New York Dr. Wright of the navy, who saw Dr. Bates shortly before his death. All concur in commending his quiet virtues, his amiability, and his professional faithfulness. In a season of prevailing and dangerous sickness in our squadron in the Gulf of Mexico, he devoted himself with entire self-forgetfulness to his duties, and assumed from sympathy and zeal those which primarily belonged to others. I understand that all the other medical gentlemen who were with him were prostrated with disease, or not immediately at hand, when he himself was seized, after most exhausting occupation, with the suffering. He died at a temporary hospital (on land) at Salmadina, Gulf of Mexico, August 26, 1847. His remains were brought home, a funeral service was held in the chapel of Mount Auburn, by his pastor, Rev. Mr. Lothrop, of Boston, and they are deposited under the monument erected to him in that cemetery."

It is worthy of mention, that, at the time of the sickness spoken of in this letter, Dr. Bates had received from Washington leave of absence. But, at Commodore Perry's request, he postponed using it, out of regard to the exigencies of others, and his own sense of duty, and thus fell a victim to the prevailing disease, which was yellow-fever.

The monument alluded to above is a handsome white-marble sarcophagus, and bears the following epitaph, written by Mr. Ellis: —

"CHARLES JARVIS BATES,

Born in Boston, Nov. 24, 1813, Graduated at Harvard University, 1833,
Served as Past Assistant Surgeon in the United States Navy,
Died in the discharge of his duties, at Salmadina, Gulf of Mexico, Aug. 26, 1847.

Beloved by the Inmates of his Home, for his filial and fraternal virtues,
Esteemed by his Companions, for the Purity of his Youth and Manhood,
His early death is deplored by those who shared with him
the Duties and the Perils
Of Professional Service, and who bear a united testimony to his
Devotion and Fidelity."

On one end of the monument a coat of arms is cut, with the motto, so appropriate in this case, —

Et manu et corde.

JOSEPH HARRINGTON, JR.

JOSEPH HARRINGTON, JR. was the son of Joseph and Mary (Smith) Harrington, and was born in Roxbury, February 21, 1813. His father was a lawyer, who practised in the counties of both Norfolk and Suffolk. His mother was the daughter of Mr. Ralph Smith, of Roxbury, at one time a noted politician of the Democratic school. After the ordinary preliminary training in his native town, he went to Exeter Academy, and passed two years there, previous to entering college. In the Class Book he pays a tribute to Dr. Abbot, of Exeter, and to Mr. Edward B. Emerson, who was one of the instructors in Roxbury. In college he maintained a respectable rank as a scholar, and graduated among the first sixteen. A letter from him to the secretary, dated Hartford, August 12, 1848, describes his course after leaving college: —

" Before I was graduated, I had entered upon my duties as

principal of Kent Academy, East Greenwich, Rhode Island. I continued in that station about six months, when I made application for a mastership in one of the grammar schools of Boston. I was successful; and about the beginning of the year 1834 commenced my career in that city as master of the Hawes Grammar School. I held this office till June, 1839. The last few years of my labors as an instructor, I was also pursuing the study of theology with Dr. Putnam of Roxbury. I preached my first sermon at Fall River, the last Sunday in June, or first in July, 1839. In the following autumn I was ordained as an evangelist in the Federal Street Church, Boston; and about the beginning of October started for Chicago, Illinois, on a short tour of missionary duty. My labors there were unexepectedly prospered. My position grew more and more interesting; and my stay there was prolonged from year to year, until the summer of 1844, when I dissolved connection with the society, leaving it prosperous and self-subsistent. I was never regularly settled over the parish in Chicago. While there, on the 6th day of April, 1841, I married Helen Euphaine Griswold, then recently from Baltimore, Maryland. The remainder of the year 1844, and the whole of 1845, I lived with my family at Roxbury, Massachusetts. During the year 1845 I officiated as pastor of the Suffolk Street Chapel, Boston. The first Sunday in January, 1846, I entered upon the duties of a new parish in Hartford, Connecticut, to the charge of which I had been invited. In April of the same year I was installed as pastor of the society. I have had three children; — one, an infant son, was buried at Chicago; another at Roxbury. Our eldest, a daughter, is living, at this date, about six and a half years of age."

Mr. Harrington remained in Hartford until the summer of 1852, and then accepted a call to take charge of the Unitarian Church at San Francisco, California. He sailed from New York on the 20th of July, and reached San Francisco on the 27th of August, after a fatiguing and suffering trip. He began, however, under bright auspices, and his church during the three Sundays on which he preached was thronged by hearers. But he was soon prostrated by illness. He had been indisposed from May of that year, — probably because of the excessive labors of the few preceding months. This indisposition was much aggravated by the exertion and excitement incident to his removal. The disease which now attacked him was pronounced Panama fever. He was taken sick early in October, and died November 2, 1852, at the age of thirty-nine.

He was much respected in his various homes after leaving college, — South Boston, Chicago, Hartford, and San Francisco, — and died regretted by a wide circle.

Such are the outlines of his successful life. They have been wrought into an interesting memoir by his classmate, William Whiting, which is prefixed to a small volume of his sermons, published by Crosby and Nichols, (Boston, 1854,) to which the class are referred. This volume contains also a good likeness.

After Mr. Harrington's death, the church at St. Francisco raised a fund for his widow and daughter. This, supplemented by lessons in music, in which Mrs. Harrington was a proficient, supported them comfortably, — particularly as the daughter, on growing up, became herself an accomplished music-teacher. So they lived in Roxbury, Mass., the home of the Harrington family; in Baltimore, where they were in 1858; and in Chicago. From the last-named place they moved to New York and made their home in Haerlem. Here Mrs. Harrington died, about ten years ago. A year or two after, the daughter, Helen Josephine, married Mr. Joseph Gandolfo, a New York gentleman of ample means. They have three children.

CHARLES HENRY PEIRCE.

CHARLES HENRY PIERCE was the son of Benjamin (H. C. 1801) and Lydia Ropes (Nichols) Peirce, and was born in Salem, January 28, 1814. His father was College Librarian, 1826-31. The great mathematician, who graduated four years before, was his elder brother.

In boyhood he was amiable and affectionate, and remarkable for his conscientiousness, love of truth, and disinterested generosity. He was quiet and observing. This faculty always remained with him, and was of great use in his professional studies and occupations.

At the age of twelve, he went to Mr. Putnam's academy, in Andover, where he remained a year. In July, 1826, he removed with his parents to Cambridge. In August, 1828, he entered Exeter Academy, and remained there a year also. In the Class Book, he bore, as so many have done, a grateful testimony to Dr. Abbot, the honored head of that institution. When nearly fitted for college, he returned to Cambridge, and, after studying a few months with Mr. Timothy Walker (H. C. 1826), entered college in December, 1829.

Here he was marked by the traits which had distinguished his boyhood. He was popular among his classmates, and had many warm friends.

Immediately after graduating, he commenced the study of medicine with Dr. G. C. Shattuck, and continued with him for three years. During the same time he attended three full courses of lectures at the Massachusetts Medical College. In August, 1836, he took the usual degrees, and then established himself at Buffalo, N. Y., as a physician. He remained there only until the beginning of 1837, and then returned to Boston, where he practised until June, 1838. Then he removed to Salem, and remained there as a medical practitioner until the middle of April, 1847, when he removed to Roxbury, where he continued to practise until the middle of September of the same year.

Dr. Peirce then relinquished medicine, and entered the chemical department of the Lawrence Scientific School, under Professor Horsford, and remained there until January 12, 1849. He was one of the first two who entered this department.

On the 21st of August, 1850, he was appointed United States Examiner of Drugs, &c. for the Port of Boston. He discharged the duties of this office with great skill and fidelity, and with characteristic fearlessness. He was removed on January 14, 1855.

In September, 1850, he superintended the translation from the German of Stockhardt's "Principles of Chemistry," published by Mr. John Bartlett, of Cambridge. This work was stereotyped, and had a very large sale. The German author has spoken of the faithfulness and spirit of the translation in terms of the highest admiration.

In March, 1852, he prepared a work entitled "Examinations of Drugs, Medicines, &c.," giving some of the results of his official labors. It was published by Mr. Bartlett, whose interest was subsequently bought by Mr. Henry C. Baird, of Philadelphia. This book was much prized, both in Europe and in this country, and commanded a large sale for a work of the kind.

Dr. Peirce died at Cambridge, after a long and painful illness, June 16, 1855, at the age of forty-one.

FREDERIC PARKER.

FREDERIC PARKER was the son of Joseph and Olive (Bailey) Parker, and was born at Carlisle, Mass., September 2, 1813. He was fitted for college at schools in the adjoining towns. At Cambridge he sustained a respectable rank as a scholar, and manifested energy and perseverance in pursuing means of improvement not prescribed by the Faculty. After graduating, he taught school in Gloucester for about nine months, then in Billerica for two years and a quarter, and lastly in Hallowell, Maine, for one year and three quarters. Early in September, 1838, he began the study of the law with Hon. Samuel Wells, of Hallowell, subsequently Judge of the Supreme Court of Maine. In September, 1839, he entered the Law School at Cambridge, where he completed his studies, and received the degree of LL. B. in 1841. He then established himself in Lowell. After spending a short time in the office of Joel Adams, Esq. (H. C. 1805), of that city, he was admitted to the bar. In October, 1844, he married Miss Harriet M. Kimball of Lowell. In 1845, he experienced a long and severe illness, the effects of which never left him, and from that time he was forced to struggle with ill health. In the same year, he was chosen one of the school committee, and held that office during four successive years. The cause of education always interested him, and during his term of office he suggested and supported several important changes in the management of the Lowell schools. In 1846 he was chosen clerk of the Salem and Lowell Railroad Company, which office he continued to fill until his last sickness. In 1849 he was instrumental in forming the Howard Fire Insurance Company, of which for several years he was secretary and treasurer. In 1852 he opened a book and print store in

Lowell, and soon after another in Boston. The former was
soon closed, and he devoted his energies to the latter. In
this employment he manifested great taste and enterprise.
In the summer of 1856, his business in Boston became
unsuccessful, and he was forced to abandon it. He then
retired to Lowell. In the autumn of that year, he had
repeated attacks of hemorrhage, and died of consumption,
January 29, 1857.

He showed through life the grave and earnest character
he displayed in college, and kept up to an unusual degree
the literary tastes which he there acquired. He encountered
reverses, but maintained through them all energy of spirit
and unsullied integrity.

His widow continued to live at Lowell, with his two surviving children, Charles Edward, born in 1848, and Frederic
Augustus, born in 1853. After the lapse of some time, Mrs.
Parker married Mr. Sidney Spalding, of Lowell, a gentleman
of wealth and liberality. He adopted her two sons, who took
his name. The eldest, Charles Parker Spalding, graduated at
Harvard in 1870, and took the degree of M. D. in 1877. In
1882, he went abroad and studied at Paris and Vienna, taking
up the eye and ear as a specialty. He is now established as
a physician in Lowell. The youngest, Frederic Parker Spalding, graduated at the Massachusetts Institute of Technology,
in 1878. He is now employed in the City Engineer's office
at Boston. In June, 1881, he married Miss Alice French, of
Lowell, and has an infant daughter, born January 19, 1883.

THOMAS BUTLER POPE.

THOMAS BUTLER POPE died at his residence in Appleton Place, Roxbury, near Longwood, January 15, 1862, aged forty-eight years lacking seven days. He was son of Lemuel and Sally Belknap (Russell) Pope, and was born in Boston, January 22, 1814. His father was a very respectable citizen, for many years President of the Boston Insurance Company. His mother was sister to the late Nathaniel Pope Russell, Esq., and second-cousin to Rev. Dr. Jeremy Belknap. He was fitted for college at the Boston Latin School, and entered at the beginning of the sophomore year. After graduating he entered the Law School of the University, and subsequently studied in the office of Hon. Charles Loring, of Boston. In the summer of 1836 he was admitted to the Suffolk Bar, and began to practise. In 1840 he formed a partnership with Charles Henry Parker (H. C. 1835), which continued until 1853, and then terminated on that gentleman becoming Treasurer of the Suffolk Savings Bank.

Though beginning the practice of law under good auspices, and in some ways manifesting proficiency, he was tempted to enter into speculations quite foreign to his profession. In this he simply followed the example of many other lawyers. But with him his ventures met with disaster, and, being continued, resulted in bankruptcy of fortune, though his integrity was unscathed. His affairs were so much embarrassed in 1858, the year when the class celebrated their "silver wedding," that he was with difficulty induced to attend the meeting. In 1859 he went into insolvency. His pecuniary misfortunes preyed upon him, and, it was thought, somewhat affected his mind for several of the last years of his life. The disease of which he finally died was softening of the brain, which began to come on, it was thought, about two years before his death. On the 1st of April, 1861, whilst driving from Boston, he was seized with an attack of paralysis, affecting his lower limbs. He was conveyed to his home, and never left it again. After lingering more than nine months, he died.

He married, June 3, 1846, Gertrude, daughter of the late John Binney, Esq., of Boston, who survived him. He left also three daughters; — Gertrude Binney, born 1847; Louisa Binney, born 1855; and Mary Binney, born 1858.

Mrs. Pope died at Boston, January 29, 1881. The eldest daughter married Bryant P. Tilden (M. I. T. 1868), and died at Phillipsburg, Montana, March 26, 1878, leaving children. The youngest died in Boston, November 21, 1876. Louisa alone survives, who is the wife of Rev. J. Frederic Dutton, of South Boston.

FLETCHER WEBSTER.

FLETCHER WEBSTER, son of the eminent statesman and orator, Daniel Webster, was born in Portsmouth, N. H., July 23, 1813. His preparatory studies having been completed at the public Latin School in Boston, he entered Harvard College in 1829, and graduated in 1833, obtaining the distinction of being chosen class orator at graduating, — an honor more gratifying to his social disposition than academic laurels.

Upon leaving college he studied law, partly with Samuel B. Walcott at Hopkinton, Mass., and partly with his father in Boston, and was in due time admitted to the Suffolk Bar and began the practice of his profession in Boston. In the autumn of 1836 he married Caroline Story, daughter of Hon. Stephen White, of Salem, Mass., and immediately after his marriage put in execution a plan previously formed of trying his profession at the West. He went first to Detroit, where he remained till the close of 1837, and then removed to La Salle, Ill., where he made the acquaintance of Abraham Lincoln, — an incident kindly recalled by the latter during his presidency, in 1861.

Notwithstanding the possession of qualities strikingly adapted to insure success in his chosen profession, Webster seems never to have contemplated with pleasure a permanent practice of the law; and when, in 1840, his father was appointed Secretary of State under President Harrison, he repaired to Washington, where the office of private secretary to Mr. Webster proved much more congenial to his tastes and temperament. The affectionate relations which subsisted between father and son during this period of mutual confidence form an interesting episode in their lives; and to his son's talent and perception Mr. Webster gladly intrusted the management of important affairs, while he found in him delightful companionship. In 1843, when the late Caleb Cushing was appointed Commissioner to China, Webster accompanied him as Secretary of Legation, returning in 1845. In 1850 he was appointed by President Taylor Surveyor of the Port of Boston, — an office which he retained until March, 1861, when a successor was nominated by President Lincoln. In these various capacities Webster manifested much practical ability, being always noted for popular qualities of mind and heart, which, though they may have retarded higher ambition, served to endear him to those with whom he was associated.

Immediately after the firing on Fort Sumter, he responded to an appeal made to the patriotic citizens of Massachusetts by the following notice, which appeared in the Boston papers of Saturday, April 20, 1861: —

". Fellow-citizens, — I have been assured by the Executive Department that the State will accept at once an additional regiment of infantry. I therefore propose to meet to-morrow at ten o'clock, in front of the Merchants' Exchange, State Street, such of my fellow-citizens as will join in raising this new regiment. The muster roll will be ready to be signed then and there. Respectfully,

"FLETCHER WEBSTER."

At the appointed hour on Sunday, April 21, an immense crowd appeared in State Street; and such was the enthusiasm produced by the meeting that in three days the muster-roll was filled; and, after various vicissitudes incident to preliminary drill, during which the discipline of the men was perfected, the regiment with full ranks joined the Army of the Potomac. Early in 1862 the regiment was ordered into Virginia for more active service, and for several months remained guarding the upper Potomac, in order to prevent the enemy from crossing into Maryland. During this time Colonel Webster displayed many of the traits of an excellent commander. His discipline was not alloyed by petulance and passion. The soldierly appearance of his men and the order of the camp gave a good name to the regiment. To use the words of his biographer, "His men were warmly attached to their colonel. They appreciated his manly frankness, his simplicity of character, his kindness of heart, and the cheerfulness with which he bore the hardships and privations of the service, though he had no longer the unworn energies of youth to sustain him."

It was while Colonel Webster was absent on leave, being called home by the death of a favorite child, that the regiment was for the first time seriously engaged, in the battle of Cedar Mountain, August 9, 1862. The behavior of the officers and men under a galling fire showed their discipline. Upon the return of Colonel Webster to his regiment, they were ordered to join McDowell's corps, under General Pope, moving toward the north fork of the Rappahannock, in order to hold the passes in that vicinity. On the 28th of August, their division, under General Ricketts, encountered General

Longstreet's advance, and were sharply engaged, Colonel Webster "behaving splendidly" according to the report of one of his officers. Two days after, on August 30, they were stationed on the left in the second battle of Bull Run, being confronted by the main force of the Rebel army. The onslaught of the enemy was fierce and irresistible. The regiment was overborne by superior numbers, and while it was falling back in good order, and without breaking ranks, Colonel Webster received a mortal wound. Lieutenant Haviland was near him when he fell, and with two men went with him to the rear. They laid him under a sheltering bush, but Lieutenant Haviland being himself shortly after taken prisoner, the wounded Colonel was left to die alone.

His body was after the battle recovered by the exertions of Lieutenant Arthur Dehon, the eldest son of his life-long and intimate friend, William Dehon. It was carried to Boston, and the funeral took place in that city on the 9th of September, 1862. It was the wish of Colonel Webster that, if he died in the war and his body was brought home, it should repose one night on the table in the library of his father's house at Marshfield. Accordingly, immediately after the funeral, a hearse, drawn by fleet black horses, and attended only by one carriage containing our classmates Dehon and Eaton, and Mr. Peter Butler, an intimate family friend, set out for that place, arriving early in the evening. His wish was reverently complied with, and the next day all that was mortal of Fletcher Webster was interred on that desolate bluff which overlooks the ocean, and where repose the remains of his father and kindred.

To quote again from his memoir, prepared for "Harvard Memorial Biographies" by George S. Hillard: "Colonel Webster was long mourned and affectionately remembered by the officers and men who had served under him. And there were others who grieved for his loss; for though not widely known, he had many faithful friends who had known and loved him from boyhood, and had stood by him in all the changes and chances of life. His own heart was warm, his nature generous and open, and his temperament cordial and frank. His tastes were strongly social, and his powers of social entertainment were such as few men possess. He had an unerring sense of the ludicrous, his wit was ready and responsive, and no man could relate an amusing incident or tell a humorous story with more dramatic power. Nor was he without faculties of a higher order. His perceptions were quick and accurate; he was an able and forcible speaker; he wrote with a clearness and strength that belonged to him by right of inheritance. The value which his friends had for him was higher than the mark which he made upon the times. The course of his life had not in all respects been favorable to his growth and influence, and he had not the iron resolution and robust purpose which makes will triumph over circumstance."

Colonel Webster was peculiarly fortunate in his death. To none was the country so much indebted as to his father for the faith that was in them in regard to the unity of the nation. When, however, in the process of events, this question drifted into war, — when that unity was at stake, and was to be settled in the dread arbitrament of battle, — then it was meet that the son of Daniel Webster should die to defend the position for which his father had contended so triumphantly, and which accorded thoroughly with his own well-grounded belief; and he died gallantly, at the head of his regiment, with his face to the foe.

Colonel Webster left a widow and three children, — two sons and one daughter. His eldest son, Daniel, died at Marshfield in 1865, at the age of twenty-five. The youngest son, Ashburton, died at New York in 1879, aged thirty. His daughter, Caroline, widow of James Geddes Day, died at Marshfield, August 16, 1881. None of these left issue.

BOLTON AND KELLY.

MOSES KELLY.

MOSES KELLY died at Cleveland, Ohio, August 15th, 1870, of pulmonary consumption, after an illness of some months.

Mr. Kelly was born at Groveland, Livingston County, New York, on the 21st of January, 1809. His father, Daniel Kelly, emigrated from Northumberland County, Pennsylvania, to the valley of the Genessee, where he bought large tracts of land and carried on a farm. His mother's maiden name was Mary Roupe, a Philadelphian of good family. He was prepared for college at the celebrated school at Temple Hill, Geneseo, N. Y., then kept by three young Harvard graduates, afterwards distinguished in their several professions, — the late Rev. Dr. Seth Sweetser of Worcester, the late President Felton, and the late Mr. Henry R. Cleveland. He was the oldest person in the class, being over twenty when he entered. The rank, however, he immediately took, was by no means due to this alone. He early showed himself a good scholar, and easily maintained throughout his college course a high standing in this respect. But what more impressed the class was a certain weight and judicial gravity of character, which made him *facile princeps* in all class gatherings.

Immediately after graduating, he entered the law office of Orlando Hastings, Esq., of Rochester, N. Y., where he read for three years. In 1836 he went to Cleveland, Ohio, and formed a partnership with his intimate friend, classmate, and college chum, Thomas Bolton. This partnership continued for twenty years, and was dissolved only by the latter being elected to a seat on the bench of the Court of Common Pleas. After the termination of this connection, Mr. Kelly continued till his death chiefly devoted to his profession. He made commercial law and equity a specialty, and as an equity lawyer was esteemed in Ohio to be one of the foremost in this country.

In 1839 he was chosen city attorney. In 1844-45 he served two years in the State Senate. "In this body," says the Cleveland Plain Dealer, "though avowedly a Whig, he maintained a manly independence, and voted against his party whenever a nice sense of right so prompted him." In September, 1866, President Johnson appointed him attorney for the Northern District of Ohio; he held the office until March following, when the Senate refused to confirm his appointment, on the ground of his having been a member of the Philadelphia Convention the previous summer.

In 1839 he married Jane, daughter of General Howe, of New Haven, Conn., an extensive publisher and book importer of that place. He had six children, of whom four, — two sons and two daughters, — with their mother, survive.[1]

In 1850 he purchased a tract of thirty acres on Euclid Avenue, in Cleveland, then known as the Giddings Farm, where he built a house which was thenceforward his home.

At a meeting of the Cuyahoga County Bar held at Cleveland, immediately after his death, the following resolutions were passed.

"In view of the recent death of Hon. Moses Kelly, the members of the bar of Cuyahoga County, here convened, adopt the following *Resolutions:* —

"1. That while we submit with humble resignation to the dispensation of Providence in removing from our midst our

[1] See note A, p. 52.

friend and brother, we can never cease to lament the loss of one who, by reason of his intellectual superiority, his careful study and training, his genial disposition, his sound judgment, became eminent in his profession, beloved and respected as a citizen, and whose death creates a void which cannot easily be filled.

"2. That in the death of Moses Kelly the bar has lost one of its most distinguished members, a man of great industry and perseverance, faithful as a friend, wise, just, and scrupulously honest as a man and counsellor, and firm and unwavering in the discharge of every duty.

"3. That we tender our deepest sympathy to the family of the deceased, and join in a body in the funeral ceremonies.

"4. That the President of this meeting be requested to communicate a copy of these resolutions to the family of the deceased, and to the Court of Common Pleas of Cuyahoga County, Ohio, and ask to have them entered on the journal of the court; and that George Willey, Esq. be a committee to present these resolutions to the District and Circuit Courts for the Northern District of Ohio, with a request that they be entered upon their journals."

These resolutions were supported by feeling and eloquent speeches; among others, the following words from Bushnel White, Esq., U. S. Commissioner, will find a response with all who have ever known Mr. Kelly: —

"Moses Kelly was too quiet, too honest, too pure and noble in character, to be a favorite subject of *earthly* eulogists in this age of greed, and pride, and ism. He loved his profession, not for the money or reputation it brought him, but for the good it enabled him to do his fellow-man. He guarded and protected the estates of widows and orphans committed to his care, to benefit them, not to enrich himself. Of the value of money, for brilliant equipage and costly entertainment, he was wholly indifferent; in feeding the hungry and clothing the naked, he was fully cognizant, as many a poor man can testify. He was not envious of the professional success of his contemporaries in the law, for he was not capable of such a feeling; he stood too high to be affected by that passion, which has dragged even angels down. Indeed, he stood pre-eminent as a chancery lawyer at this bar. Nor was this wonderful. His entire uprightness, his perfect purity of character, ever leading him to love equity and do equity, taught him to know equity. He has gone where not a single principle governing him for sixty-two years of earthly existence will need change to bring him safely through that narrow gate which leads to life eternal."

Other speakers laid stress on the great strength of intellect shown by Mr. Kelly, and on his uncommon modesty. To his influence, also, was largely ascribed the courtesy between attorneys observable at the Cleveland Bar.

In presenting the above resolutions to the United States Circuit Court, Mr. Willey, in the course of his remarks, said: "Of unquestioned and recognized ability as a lawyer, and especially learned in at least one great department of the law, it was true of him, that high above professional achievement and success rose his character as a *man*."

THOMAS BOLTON.

THOMAS BOLTON died suddenly at Cleveland, Ohio, February 1st, 1871, of neuralgia of the heart. He was born at Scipio, Cayuga County, N. Y., where his father was an extensive farmer, on the 29th of November, 1809. He was prepared for college at Geneseo, N. Y., at the same school and under the same distinguished masters as his friend, the subject of the previous notice, and entered with him after the winter vacation, in February, 1830. He had a respectable rank as a scholar, and took a lively interest and a prominent part in all that concerned the class. Before he left Cambridge it was felt that his incisive character and great energy would make his presence felt wherever he finally found a home.

Upon graduating, he read law rather more than a year in the office of John C. Spencer, Esq., at Canandaigua, N. Y. Then, after due travel and deliberation, he finally selected Cleveland, Ohio, as his residence, where he established himself in the autumn of 1834, and was admitted to the bar in September, 1835. After remaining in connection with James L. Conger, Esq., for about a year, he sent for his classmate and life-long friend, Moses Kelly, and the two formed a partnership in the autumn of 1836. This connection continued for twenty years, having a leading position in the northern part of Ohio, and lasting until 1856, when Mr. Bolton was elected one of the judges of the Court of Common Pleas. This office he held for ten years. After his retirement from the bench, in 1866, he devoted himself to his private affairs. He had amassed a fortune, the care of which occupied his time.

Judge Bolton married, September 7, 1837, Elizabeth L. Cone, who died January 26, 1846, having had five children, four of whom — three sons and one daughter — are living. December 1, 1846, he married Emeline Russell, who, with one of her sons, survives.[1] He lived on Euclid Avenue, the great ornament of the suburbs of Cleveland, at a place adjoining that of Mr. Kelly, and in a house exactly like that of his friend. He always maintained interest in his Alma Mater, and of his four sons three have been Harvard students.

In the Cleveland Daily Leader of February 2, 1871, may be found the following: "Few men in this community are so widely known as Judge Bolton. His long prominence as

[1] See note B, p. 52.

a lawyer, judge, politician, and man of wealth, made him known among all classes, and if candor requires it to be said that he had enemies, it is equally true to say that he had his portion of friends. As a man he had peculiarities that did not contribute to his popularity with the masses, his manner being generally cold and often even stern; but behind this external crust of seeming harshness those who could touch him nearest knew there lived a warm heart and a genial nature, and to his friends, and particularly in the circle of his home, he was the most companionable and social of men. As a lawyer, when in the full tide of his practice, he was the peer of the ablest of his contemporaries. The firm of Kelly and Bolton held, during its existence, a leading and enviable position. As a judge he was fearless and impartial, looking only to the side of justice, whether the issue affected the lowly or the great, the poor or the rich. In his private dealings he was distinguished by a strict integrity and a faithful adherence to his engagements, and the well-defined principles which governed his conduct in this regard he exacted of others. In every position he brought to his work untiring energy, indomitable perseverance, and the will to succeed. The marked success of his life bears the best testimony to his ability and his sagacity."

At a meeting of the Cleveland Bar, held a day or two after Judge Bolton's death, the following resolutions were unanimously adopted: —

"*Whereas*, It has pleased God to remove by death Thomas Bolton, a distinguished member of this bar; and

"*Whereas*, The members of this bar desire publicly to express their sense of the loss sustained by them in this dispensation of Divine Providence; therefore be it

"*Resolved*, That Judge Bolton, by devotion to the duties of his profession, by observing and maintaining under all circumstances the true relations which exist between the lawyer and his client, by his integrity, his ability, and the aid and encouragement given by him to young men, has afforded us an example worthy of commendation and imitation.

"*Resolved*, That his career as a judge of this district was marked by that devotion to duty, that regard for the right of suitors, and that independence and impartiality, which commanded the respect and approval of the profession and of this community.

"*Resolved*, That in all the walks of life, whether as a citizen, a counsellor, or a friend, or in the more intimate relations of social and domestic life, we have ever found him in the highest degree exemplary, faithful to his obligations, and true to his profession.

"*Resolved*, That we will ever cherish his memory with that affection which a life true to its high duties, a professional career devoted to its noblest purposes, and intercourse with us for years marked by kindness and integrity, necessarily inspire.

"*Resolved*, That we tender his family our warmest sympathies in their sore bereavement, and ask the privilege of following his remains to the grave, as those bereaved of a friend and brother.

"*Resolved*, That the chairman of this meeting be requested to move the Court of Common Pleas, at its next session, to place these resolutions on the records of said court, and that Hon. George Willey be requested to procure the same action in the United States Court for this district, and that a copy of them be sent to the family of our departed brother."

These resolutions were followed by several speeches eulogistic of the deceased. Among others, Judge J. P. Bishop spoke of him as a judge, as follows: —

"But Judge Bolton was not only the successful lawyer and eminent man I have before spoken of, but he was honored by being elected twice as Judge of the Court of Common

Pleas. It was in this capacity I best knew him. And here let me say that, as a lawyer, it was faithfulness to his client's interest that was a great distinction in his character, and when he was on the bench it was his impartial, unflinching determination to administer the law as applicable to the testimony that was the most distinguishing feature of his judicial character.

"These characteristics at the bar and on the bench made him appear at times arbitrary; but when one came to know him, they would readily see he was only carrying out what he deemed was his duty to client and litigant. But he was not arbitrary in any natural sense; it was rather apparent than otherwise. I had occasion to know him intimately in our associations together on the bench, and in all our private consultations and deliberations, officially, at home; and on the circuit, no person was more desirous to get at the exact truth and right than he, and no person was more ready to yield an opinion the moment he came to see that he was mistaken.

"Judge Bolton had this distinguishing trait of character, — that of positiveness, — and this I observed more on the bench than anywhere else, and it had in many cases a very useful result, — that was to quiet litigation."

Thus lived and died the subject of the last notice and of the preceding one. "Bolton and Kelly" were household words for the four years of their college life, and have continued so with scores of their classmates and college friends. Their whole connection was remarkable. Coming to Cambridge, towards the close of 1829, from the same birthplace, Western New York, and the same preparatory school, — of nearly the same age and five years older than the average of their classmates, — they at once took a stand higher than that belonging to simple seniority. Inseparable through their college life, parted only in their professional preparation, they came together again, three years after graduating, in the city of Cleveland, to form a partnership which continued for twenty years, and was eminent throughout a wide territory, and to resume a friendship which lasted until death, in which event they were separated by a space of less than six months.

This life-long intimacy was the more remarkable, because of the wide difference in the characters of the two. Their tastes, motives, and habits of mind, indeed, were not only wholly unlike, but diametrically opposite. Mr. Kelly was a churchman and a conservative; Judge Bolton, a radical in church and state. The former had much benevolence, the latter much thriftiness. Mr. Kelly possessed trained powers of thought and learning; Judge Bolton, homely commonsense and sagacity. Each was consistent and faithful to his ideal.

Very seldom can Harvard expect to send out two graduates, who, from their long and unbroken harmony and rare blending of opposite virtues, are able to affect a wider circle or leave a deeper impression.

NOTE A.

CHILDREN OF MOSES AND JANE (HOWE) KELLY.

Frank Howe, born May 21, 1840; attorney at law, Cleveland, Ohio; three years at Kenyon College; married, and has two children; — a son, living with him; and a daughter, married in January, 1883, to J. C. Barney, of New York.

Jane Eliza, born Jan. 28, 1842; died January, 1872.

George D., born November, 1844; educated at Western Reserve College; married November, 1871, and has three children; now resides in Pennsylvania, and is in the iron business.

Margaret S., born June 16, 1846; lives with her mother.

Mary, born July, 1848; died July, 1863.

Clara, born June, 1850; married Earle J. Knight, of Ann Arbor, Michigan, December, 1879, and has one son.

Mrs. Moses Kelly lives in Cleveland, on the old place, but not in the old homestead.

NOTE B.

CHILDREN OF THOMAS AND ELIZABETH L. (CONE) BOLTON.

Festus Cone, born June 7, 1838; died Feb. 8, 1839.

Thomas Kelly, born March 25, 1840; graduated at Harvard, 1861; a lawyer by profession; died of hemorrhage of the brain, July 10, 1879.

Elizabeth Cone, born Aug. 16, 1841; married, and has two sons; lives in Brunswick, Germany, where she has been settled for ten years.

Festus Cone, born Jan. 12, 1844; lives as a farmer in Leicester, N. Y.; married, and has two children, — one son and one daughter.

James Henry, born Jan. 20, 1846; educated at Western Reserve College, 1866; LL. B. at Harvard, 1869; is Clerk of the Court in Sioux City, Iowa; has been in the Iowa Legislature; married, but has no children.

CHILDREN OF THOMAS AND EMELINE (RUSSELL) BOLTON.

George Russell, born Jan. 31, 1851; died Sept. 9, 1859.

Charles Chester, born March 23, 1855; was some time a student in the class of 1878, H. C.; lives with his mother in the old homestead at Cleveland, Ohio; is in the wholesale iron trade; married, and has one son.

CHARLES JACKSON.

CHARLES JACKSON was the son of Charles and Fanny (Cabot) Jackson, and was born in Boston, March 4, 1815. His father, a distinguished jurist, was on the bench of the Supreme Court of Massachusetts from 1813 to 1823, and during a long life commanded the respect and reverence of the entire community.

He was fitted for college chiefly at the schools of Mr. Daniel Greenleaf Ingraham and Mr. William Wells. Somewhat retired from his fellows, he devoured books, constructed curious machines, discussed grave questions, and in various ways showed the remarkable acuteness and versatility which distinguished his later life.

Entering college at the beginning of the sophomore year, at Commencement, 1830, he was soon recognized as the genius of the class. He disregarded college rank, satisfied in this respect with being admitted among the second "eight" to the Phi Beta Kappa Society. His time as an undergraduate was devoted to desultory reading, principally in English belles-lettres, and the fascinations of chemistry.

After graduating he began the study of the law with his father, and continued it in the office of Hon. Charles G. Loring. He was admitted to the Suffolk Bar in 1836. The years 1837 and 1838 he spent in Europe. On returning, he attended to civil engineering, which he prosecuted on the Western and Eastern railroads in Massachusetts during the years 1839 and 1840. His natural tastes and talents, largely mechanical, well fitted him for the last-named profession; and his remarkable quickness of mind and immense fund of miscellaneous knowledge would have rendered him eminent in the former. But after 1840 he abandoned both, and turned his attention to iron-making, styling himself thenceforward an "iron-master."

After passing through a season of disaster and surmounting it, his ability made his tasks so light that he found ample leisure for various studies, which almost to the last had an ever-increasing attraction, and for that simple and hearty hospitality which for a quarter of a century delighted its favored recipients, whether they were the distinguished of this or other lands, or simply old friends with little learning or talent.

He married, February 16, 1842, his cousin, Susan C., youngest daughter of the late Dr. James Jackson, who survives him.

He died in Boston, July 30, 1871, after a lingering and painful illness of many months.

He left two sons and one daughter. His eldest child married the Rev. George McKean Folsom, and died a short time before him, leaving one daughter. The sons are successful stockbrokers in Boston. The eldest is married and has children. They both graduated at Harvard.

The following biographical notice of him appeared in the columns of the Boston Daily Advertiser, a few days after his death.

" After a long-protracted illness, endured with uncomplaining patience, Mr. Charles Jackson, the second of that name, son of the eldest of the three brothers Charles, James, and Patrick, all very honored and well remembered in our community, has laid down the burden of a suffering life. He was less known to the world than many men of his force of mind and character, having cared little for any distinction he might have gained by the display of his remarkable abilities. Except on a single occasion, the delivery of a lecture in a course instituted by the American Academy, he has hardly been before the public at all. Those who remember the freshness and originality of that effort know with what effect he could handle facts and arguments, and can judge how powerful an advocate and how dangerous an opponent he would have shown himself in any discussion into which he might have thrown his swift and subtle intelligence.

"But his business was a practical one, and he was content to devote his energies mainly to building up that large manufacturing establishment which owes its existence mainly to his enterprise. The difficulties of his early career would have disheartened and broken any but a strong and brave man. His indomitable will and steady courage carried him through the season of doubt and danger, and left him, worn by an amount of overwork which doubtless shortened his life, to enjoy his remaining years in that happy home where he found his chief pleasure. In that home and the circle of immediate friends he was the centre of a love and an admiration such as few can hope to claim. He loved so well to see others happy, and knew so well how to make them so, especially the young, in whose company he always delighted, that he was sure of their affection in return. His conversation must of necessity have gained him admirers, for it was of a very rare and fascinating quality. He was full of knowledge on a great variety of subjects, pointed and penetrating in statement, keen in argument, in which he seldom found his match, copious in expression, affluent in resources, an iconoclast among the commonplaces of ignorant belief, to whom it was always wholesome to listen. His letters were as remarkable as his conversation. He went straight to the heart of his subject, with the directness of a telegraphic message. He would shake a question to pieces in less time than most men would take to make a statement of it. His wonderful memory, of which remarkable facts are recorded, his very wide range of reading, which with him meant getting out of a book all that was in it, his use of words for their sense, and not for sound or show, give a solid significance to all his letters on matters that interested him, — letters often written so hastily that each page blurred half the preceding one as it was folded back, and yet marrowy with meaning from the half-illegible address to the blotted initials which stood for his signature. There are more able men that do not take the trouble to be famous than the world thinks or dreams. There are more heroic lives than biographers to tell of them. This was a man of strong and searching intellect, of heroic force in the day of trial, and of very many endearing personal traits which will live in memory as long as those who loved him."

H.

HENRY YANCEY GRAY.

THE following notice of Henry Yancey Gray was written by his fellow-townsman, intimate friend, and college chum, George Inglis Crafts. The subject of it had a peculiar charm of manner, which those who knew him in Cambridge must freshly remember.

Born November 23, 1813; educated at grammar school of Charleston College, Charleston, S. C.; admitted freshman same college, where he remained until senior year, when Crafts and himself determined to go to Cambridge; entered in 1831 junior class Harvard University; graduated in 1833; returned to Charleston, and commenced studying law; was admitted to the bar, December 16, 1838; served in one of the volunteer companies which went from Charleston to St. Augustine for its defence, at the commencement of the Seminole war, as sergeant of his company; was appointed, November 22, 1839, United States District Clerk for South Carolina; occupied this position until the State seceded, and the court became the Confederate State District Court, in which he retained his position until the dissolution of the Confederacy and the court with it. When the United States and its District Court were reconstructed, he became assistant to the clerk then appointed, in which position he remained until his death, in 1872.

He was married to Miss Elizabeth Cart, in April, 1840. She died many years previous to his own death, leaving no issue. He never married again.

He himself, after many months of failing health, died in Charleston on the 4th of July, 1872.

His remains were attended to their last resting-place by many friends and acquaintances, all of whom could have borne testimony to his gentle, winning manners and genuine originality of thought. He was too modest and unobtrusive ever to have attained public honors in this rough and half-civilized country of ours, nor did he ever seek them.

His death was put down by the physicians as arising from nervous prostration.

WILLIAM WHITING.

WILLIAM WHITING was the son of William and Hannah (Conant) Whiting, and descended from Rev. Samuel Whiting, minister of the church in Lynn, whose wife was the daughter of Rt. Hon. Oliver St. John, Chief Justice of England in Cromwell's time.

Born in Concord, March 3, 1813, he pursued his preparatory studies in the academy of that town, and graduated at Harvard College in 1833. He was third scholar, Professors Bowen and Torry being before, and Professor Lovering just after him.

After graduating, he took charge of a school for young ladies in Plymouth. Remaining there about a year, he returned to Concord, where he taught a similar school. In the autumn of 1835 he entered the office of Ellis Gray Loring, counsellor at law, Boston, where he remained a year and a half. Then, after travelling for a few months in the West, he entered the Law School at Cambridge, where he took his degree as LL. B. in 1838. Admitted to the Boston Bar in November of the same year, he opened an office in Court Street in that city.

In the Court of Common Pleas his talents and industry at once commanded attention and respect, and enabled him to achieve early and enduring success, his pre-eminence being illustrated by the term "Whiting's court" often then applied to that tribunal.

He was soon prompted, however, to seek a wider field of activity in the higher courts of this and other States, and of the United States. In these, he attained his chief eminence from his success in important suits arising under the patent laws. To these cases he devoted years of careful research, and in them he developed great mechanical aptness. The minutiæ of questions to which they gave rise were scrupulously examined, and no pains spared to insure a thorough command of the case in hand. In this manner he acquired the confidence of his clients, and won for himself a distinction seldom equalled in this department of his profession, together with a fortune.

Although Mr. Whiting was much absorbed in his profession, yet, when the great crisis of the nation approached, he was especially interested in the legal and constitutional questions which were forced into prominence. He was one of the first among lawyers to claim for the United States full belligerent rights against those who inhabited the States in rebellion. His views on this subject were subsequently incorporated in his work on War Powers under the Constitution of the United States, which, says his biographer,[1] "contributed more than any other single agency to the solution of many of the difficult questions arising in the course of the war."

"The early editions of the work," says the same memoir, "were adopted by the President and the Departments as an

[1] The late Mr. Delano A. Goddard.

authority on the questions treated in it, and new editions followed as rapidly as new questions called for examination and decision. The value placed upon it is best attested by the remarkable fact, that within a period of eight years forty-three [1] editions were printed."

In November, 1862, Mr. Whiting was requested by the President to act as solicitor and special counsellor of the War Department, and this office, created by statute in 1863, he filled until the end of the war.

Mr. Whiting's first public service after the war was that of Presidential Elector in 1868, when he gave the vote of his district for General Grant. In 1872, he was elected to the Forty-third Congress. He was so equipped for this post, that he must have taken a high place in its councils. He had at command much learning. He spoke easily and with force. He had been very successful in the courts. He was used to affairs, and accustomed to influence men in high stations. Above all, his capacity for patient and effective work was immense.

But death, who seeks alike the distinguished and the humble, suddenly struck him down, in the midst of his usual health and of the high anticipations of his position.

He died at his house on Montrose Avenue, Roxbury, on the 29th of June, 1873, aged sixty years. He had been confined within doors but a few days, and his illness excited no apprehensions. Late in the afternoon of that day, whilst resting quietly on his pillow, he was seized with sharp pains about the heart, and expired in a few moments.

He was married in October, 1840, to Lydia Cushing Russell, daughter of the Hon. Thomas Russell of Plymouth, who with three children — two sons and one daughter — survived him.

Mrs. Whiting died May 7, 1881. Miss Whiting resides in

[1] To which may be added that at least one edition was prepared for foreign distribution.

Boston. The eldest son lives at Barre, Mass. The youngest, Harold, graduated at Harvard in 1877, the fourth in his class, took the following year the degree of A. M., and is now an assistant teacher at the University in the department of Physics.

Mr. Whiting by his will left five thousand dollars to Harvard College, for a scholarship.

At the end of the biography referred to above, which was prepared for the Historic Genealogical Society, there is appended a list of Mr. Whiting's separate publications, thirty-two in number, mostly legal and political, partly historical.

JEFFRIES WYMAN.

JEFFRIES WYMAN, son of Rufus and Ann (Morrill) Wyman, was born at Chelmsford, Mass., August 11, 1814. His father was the first physician of the McLean Asylum for the Insane, the earliest institution of the kind in New England. He was prepared for college at Phillips Academy, Exeter. Professor Bowen, a schoolmate, says of him while there, "He *would* take long rambles in the woods, and go into water or a-fishing, and draw funny outline sketches in his school-books, and whittle out gimcracks with his penknife, and pitch stones or a ball farther and higher than any boy in the Academy, when he ought to have been studying his lessons." He adds, "The boy was very like the man, only with age, as was natural, he became more earnest, persistent, and methodical."[1] He entered Harvard College in 1829, completing the regular course and graduating in 1833. He took no rank as a scholar, and his name does not even appear among the thirty-three who had " parts " at Commencement.

[1] Contained in a memoir of Professor Wyman, by Dr. O. W. Holmes, in the Atlantic Monthly for November, 1874.

The bent of his mind was, however, early manifested, and while he was yet an undergraduate much of his time was spent in the dissection and preparation of anatomical specimens.

The profession of medicine seemed to offer him an opportunity for the continued pursuit of his favorite occupations, and under the guidance of Dr. John Call Dalton and the counsel of his own father, himself a physician of eminence, he made noted progress, taking his medical degree in 1837. Dr. Wyman seems never to have entered on the practice of his profession, which appeared to have no more charms for him than for Agassiz and Gray. But as a teacher he was devoted to the numerous medical students who afterwards entered his laboratory. His remarkable promise as a student, however, was quickly recognized. His first appointment, after he had taken his medical degree, was as Demonstrator to Dr. John Collins Warren, the Hersey Professor of Anatomy and Surgery in Harvard University, whose chair he was destined to fill. Soon after, he received the appointment of Curator of the Lowell Institute. In 1841, he delivered a course of lectures before the Institute, and with the money received for this service he was enabled to visit Europe for the purpose of pursuing his favorite branches of study. He gave his time chiefly to the study of human and comparative anatomy, and natural history and physiology, attending the lectures of the most distinguished masters of Paris and London. He was thus busied when the news of his father's death summoned him back to his home. In 1843, he was appointed Professor of Anatomy and Physiology in the Medical Department of Hampden Sydney College, Richmond, Va. This position he resigned in 1847, at which time he was chosen Hersey Professor of Anatomy at Harvard University. To illustrate two lectures, he began the formation of that Museum of Comparative Anatomy to which the best energies of his life were devoted, and which to-day remains the most eloquent memorial of his skill and industry.

Nothing can convey so good an impression of Professor Wyman's life for the next twenty years as the following extract from the Memoir by Dr. Holmes referred to above.

"He made several voyages, partly, at least, with the object of making additions to his collections; one in 1849 to Labrador, where he came into relation with the Esquimaux and learned something of their mode of living.

"In the spring of 1833, while a senior in college, he had suffered from a dangerous attack of pneumonia, which seems to have laid the foundation of the pulmonary affection that kept him an invalid and ended by causing his death. The state of his health made it necessary for him to seek a warmer climate, and in 1852 he went to Florida, which he continued to visit during many subsequent years; for the last time during the spring of 1874. Besides these annual migrations, he revisited Europe in 1854 and 1870, and made a voyage to Surinam in 1856, and one to La Plata in 1858.

"All these excursions and seasons of exile, rendered necessary by illness, were made tributary to his scientific enterprise. His Museum kept on steadily growing, and the students who worked under his direction or listened to his lectures, the associations with which he was connected, and the scientific journals, reaped the rich fruit of his observations and his investigations during these frequent and long periods of absence.

"So he went on working for about twenty years, quietly, happily, not stimulated by loud applause, not striking the public eye with any glitter to be seen afar off, but with a mild halo about him which was as real to those with whom he had his daily walk and conversation, as the nimbus around a saint's head in an altar-piece."

It was near the end of these twenty years, in 1866, that Mr. George Peabody laid the foundation of an archæological and ethnological museum. The position of Curator was offered to Professor Wyman, and he entered with the enthusiasm of youth upon its duties. This office, and that of Hersey Professor of Anatomy, he held until the time of his death.

From 1856 to 1870, when the state of his health forced him to resign, he held the office of President of the Boston Society of Natural History. In 1857 he was chosen President of the American Association for the Promotion of Science. He never courted such honors, — they came to him unsought.

In August, 1874, after putting both his museums in perfect order, Dr. Wyman went to the White Mountains. He had experienced several slight attacks of bleeding, and when temporarily at Bethlehem he had a sudden and copious hemorrhage, which proved fatal, on Friday, September 4. On the next Tuesday his funeral services were held at Appleton Chapel in Cambridge, and he was interred at Mount Auburn. The following classmates acted as pall-bearers: Welch, Whitney, Prichard, H. W. Torrey, Bowen, Lovering, and Higginson.

At the next meeting of the Boston Society of Natural History, of which Dr. Wyman had been so long President, Dr. Asa Gray delivered a memorial address, in the course of which, after stating that Dr. Wyman was a believer in the theory of evolution, he said, " Holding to this theory, he was an earnest Theist, and a devout and habitual attendant upon Christian worship, and the psalm, 'The heavens declare the glory of God,' had never more fitting place at funeral service than when the words were said over Jeffries Wyman." At the conclusion of the address, the following resolutions were adopted.

"*Resolved*, That in the death of Jeffries Wyman the Boston Society of Natural History mourns the loss of a most honored member and efficient officer, — one who was untiring in his labors for the society during his long and active connection with it as Curator, Secretary, and President; and that in his death science has lost a most thorough and careful investigator, and the cause of education and truth a most devoted and conscientious disciple.

"*Resolved*, That as members of a society who gave to Professor Wyman the highest honor and position we could bestow, we acknowledge our indebtedness to him for the thoroughness and care with which he guided our labors for so many years, and, while filled with sorrow at our own loss, we ask the privilege, by transmission of these resolutions, of extending our sympathy to his bereaved family in their great trial."

At a meeting of the Board of Overseers held, a few weeks after Dr. Wyman's death, in Memorial Hall, Cambridge, the Hon. Charles Francis Adams, President of the Board, in the chair, Dr. Edward H. Clarke, from a committee appointed at the previous meeting, submitted the following tribute to Professor Wyman, which was adopted and ordered to be entered on their records.

"The Overseers of Harvard College desire to express their sense of the great loss which the University, the cause of science, and the community have sustained in the death of Dr. Jeffries Wyman.

"They recognize in him a man whose uprightness of character, singleness of aim, purity of manners, and devotion to duty, presented to the community in which he lived a noble example of a life well spent.

"Science found in him an ardent, patient, intelligent, and loyal disciple. Indefatigable in the pursuit of truth, successful in tracing nature's hidden footsteps, conscientious in drawing conclusions from his investigations, modest to a degree rarely known in asserting his rightful claims as a scientific discoverer, he was unexcelled as a comparative anatomist. His researches have increased the sum of human knowledge.

"As a teacher he earned and deserved not only the respect but the admiration of those he instructed, and to whom he communicated with singular success something of his own constant and impartial love of truth. His labors have honored and enriched the University.

"*Resolved*, That in grateful remembrance of his character and services, this tribute to his memory be placed upon the records of the Board of Overseers, and that a copy of it be transmitted to his family."

The following lines appeared in "The Nation" for October, 1874.

JEFFRIES WYMAN,

Died September 4, 1874.

THE wisest man could ask no more of Fate
Than to be simple, modest, manly, true,
Safe from the Many, honored by the Few;
Nothing to court in World, or Church, or State;
But inwardly in secret to be great;
To feel mysterious Nature ever new,
To touch, if not to grasp, her endless clew,
And learn by each discovery how to wait;
To widen knowledge and escape the praise;
Wisely to teach, because more wise to learn;
To toil for Science, not to draw men's gaze,
But for her lore of self-denial stern;
That such a man could spring from our decays
Fans the soul's nobler faith until it burn.   J. R. L.

Professor Wyman married, December 19, 1850, Adeline, daughter of William and Susan C. Wheelwright, of New York, and, secondly, August 15, 1861, Annie Williams, daughter of Benjamin Duick (H. C. 1828) and Elizabeth (Williams) Whitney. His first wife died June 25, 1855, leaving two daughters, — Susan, born September 15, 1851, and Mary Morrill, born May 15, 1855. The second wife died February 20, 1864, leaving one son, Jeffries, born February 3, 1864.

Any notice of Jeffries Wyman, designed for the class, should not fail to mention the constant interest he felt for his classmates.

A year after our pleasant gathering at Professor Bowen's house on the Commencement of 1867, Wyman sent the following note to the Secretary: "I shall be proud to have my Laboratory at the disposal of the class on Commencement day, if anatomical associations are not too much for them. Clary, the colored 'Mills,' who cooled our cider for us two years ago, will, I have no doubt, be glad to officiate again in the same capacity, and will insure, as far as in him lies, 'quod bonum, faustum, felixque sit,' being well served." Accordingly, that year, and in 1869, 1870, and 1871, those of us who were in Cambridge met there. In 1872, the Secretary being in Europe, no meeting took place. But in 1873 these gatherings were resumed. Since Professor Wyman's death, however, none have been held. No one who was present at these reunions can ever forget the affectionate cordiality of his greeting.

WILLIAM DEHON.

WILLIAM DEHON was born in Boston, February 2, 1814. He was the son of William and Betsey (Bicker) Dehon, and nephew of Bishop Dehon of South Carolina (H. C. 1795). On the father's side he was of French descent.

He was fitted for college at the Boston Latin School, under Benjamin Apthorp Gould (H. C. 1814), of whom he used to speak with affection and respect. He entered Harvard College in the class of 1833; but having failed to pay his college dues within the prescribed time, in consequence of a sudden summons to the death-bed of his youngest brother, he did not take his degree with the class. The degree was however given him after a year's delay.

At Harvard, he had the advantage of an early development of extremely good manners. This gave him an influence in class gatherings always attendant upon this accomplishment. To it he owed in part his election as President of the Institute of 1770. He was Librarian of the Porcellian Club, and always one of the leaders in that coterie, — between whom and the Hasty Pudding Club there were then "no dealings."

His scholarship was sufficiently good to enable him to have Parts at the two exhibitions and at Commencement. At the Junior Exhibition (Oct. 18, 1831), he took the part of Brutus in a Latin dialogue.

A Dialogue in Latin. "Cæsar, Brutus, and Flavius."
LUTHER CLARK, Waltham.
WILLIAM DEHON, <i>Boston.</i>
THOMAS WIGGLESWORTH, <i>Boston.</i></div>

His position on the programme of the Senior Exhibition (Oct. 16, 1832) indicates an improvement in rank: —

A Forensic Disputation. "Whether the Utilitarian Character of the Present Age be more conducive to Intellectual Improvement than the Chivalrous Character of the Middle Ages."
WILLIAM DEHON, Boston.
HENRY YANCEY GRAY, <i>Charleston, S. C.</i></div>

His position on the Commencement programme (Aug. 28, 1833) indicates still higher rank; but he did not speak.

A Literary Discussion. "The Poet of an Early Age and of a Civilized one."
WILLIAM DEHON, Boston.
CHARLES ALFRED WELCH, <i>Boston.</i></div>

While in college, his father failed in business, on account of the dishonesty of others, and died shortly afterwards.

In consequence he was in straitened circumstances during the latter part of his college course and for some years afterwards.

Immediately after leaving college he entered as a student the law office of Hon. Charles G. Loring. There he displayed such marked ability, that, on being admitted to the Suffolk Bar (July, 1836), he was taken into partnership. During all this time, and afterwards, he was the head of his widowed mother's house, making himself responsible for her comfort and that of his sisters, and as soon as possible contributing largely to their support.

The new partnership — then composed of Messrs. C. G. and F. C. Loring and William Dehon — in which the last remained till the summer of 1844 — did more business than any other law firm in Boston, save perhaps that of Messrs. C. P. and B. R. Curtis.

In 1844 Dehon opened an office by himself. For the next fifteen years he enjoyed a large practice of the best kind. Concerning much of his subsequent career, Mr. John D. Bryant, who became his partner, writes a letter, from which the following extracts are taken.

"My first acquaintance with Mr. Dehon was in the fall of 1854, when I became a law student in his office. He was then at the height of his professional success, and was enjoying the rewards of a well-earned reputation. The judicial qualities of his mind caused him to be largely sought for, at this period, as a referee. In this capacity, he aided in the decision, out of court, within the first five years of the writer's acquaintance with him, of causes of great commercial importance and involving large sums of money. This practice was not of a kind to bring him prominently before the public, or to win for him popular applause. But it brought him what he valued more, the reputation, with the profession and with laymen conversant with the profession, of a sound lawyer and a discriminate judge. The writer has been told by one who recently occupied the highest judicial position in this Commonwealth, and who now sits on the bench of the highest court in the nation, that Mr. Dehon might long ago have held a place on our Supreme Bench had he been so disposed. His work was done with the facility indicative of genius, rather than with the tedious toil of the plodder. His written productions, such as opinions and legal instruments, were at the same time distinguished by a clear comprehension of the principles involved, and by terseness and accuracy of expression."

The only public civil service of Dehon was as one of the Convention of 1853, to revise the Constitution of Massachusetts, — an assembly distinguished by the high character of its members.

Dehon had married, December 26, 1839, Caroline Maria Inches, daughter of Henderson Inches, a well-known citizen of Boston. She possessed great beauty, and singular loveliness of character. She died December 29, 1859, leaving two sons and one daughter. After her death his own health gave way, and he never again attempted the harder work of his profession. Mrs. Dehon's serious illness for the last two years of her life had withdrawn him from his office and business cares. "I seem," he said to Mr. Bryant, "compelled to choose whether I will neglect my profession or my wife; and it certainly shall not be my wife."

"From the death of Mrs. Dehon," adds Mr. Bryant, "Mr. Dehon seemed to lose interest in his profession. He sought relief from his afflictions in rural pursuits, devoting much of his time to horticulture, and making for himself and family a suburban home in Quincy."

From 1858 to 1864 he was interested in the Quincy Horse Railroad, of which he was President and a large stockholder. It proved, however, more profitable to the public than to the owners.

His political idol had always been Daniel Webster. He

believed his teachings fully sanctioned the maintenance of the Union at any cost. So, when Fort Sumter was fired upon, he sided with the government in its efforts to put down the rebellion. It was not long before opportunity offered for him to render great service to the national cause.

April 20, 1861, Fletcher Webster undertook to raise an additional regiment for the war. An enthusiastic meeting was held the next day in State Street, Boston, though it was Sunday, to take measures for raising "the Webster Regiment." Into this design Dehon threw himself with great ardor, and was put at the head of the Executive Committee appointed at the meeting.

He had been from boyhood the intimate friend of the gallant man who, at forty-seven, proposed to enter upon the hardships and dangers of campaign life, and well did he respond at this crisis to the calls of friendship and patriotism.

Mr. John D. Bryant, who was at that time in the best position for knowledge, speaking of Dehon's labors before the regiment was mustered into service, says: —

"He generally did all that man could do for the organization and success of the regiment. The amount of his pecuniary contributions, first and last, to it, I cannot state; but if time is money, I think he gave more than any other, almost more than all others."

Besides giving thus of his time and energy, he sent to the field his eldest son Arthur, who first served as Lieutenant in the 12th (Webster) Regiment. In this capacity, after the second battle of Bull Run, where Colonel Webster fell, this young officer returned to the field, at imminent risk to himself, and succeeded in finding the body. He buried it with his own hands, but afterwards, having obtained an ambulance, went back, and removed it. Its subsequent transmission to Boston was then procured by the untiring efforts of Lieutenant Dehon, without which, his biographer (Mr. O. W. Holmes, Jr.) writes, it would never have been sent.

It was fit that the son should thus piously perform the last services for one to whom the father had been so devoted. Three months afterwards, that son himself fell at Fredericksburg, while serving on the staff of General Meade, and when carrying an important order for his commander.

In 1867 Dehon lost his youngest son, Henderson, then a Senior at Harvard, who died in Boston after a short illness. He was a young man of great promise, whose death was sincerely mourned by all who knew him.

In 1871 Dehon went to Europe with his only surviving child, (the wife of Prof. A. S. Hill, of Cambridge,) and her family. Returning in 1873, he lived a retired life in Boston till his death, May 20, 1875.

JOHN OSGOOD STONE.

JOHN O. STONE was born in Salem, Mass., February 1, 1813. His father was Robert Stone, for many years an East India merchant in that town. His mother was Rebecca, daughter of Captain John Osgood, also a merchant of the same place.

Dr. Stone was prepared for college at the Salem Latin School, and entered Harvard in 1829.

He was a respectable scholar at Cambridge, and had a part at graduation. William M. Prichard says of him: —

" Dr. Stone had in college a certain bluff sincerity, which he retained through life. . . . He was not ambitious of mere college distinction, devoting himself to such studies as suited his tastes and purposes, rather than attempting to master the whole prescribed routine of the University."

After graduating he entered the Harvard Medical School, and in commencing the study of the profession of his choice he showed new zeal and increased diligence, because his heart was in the work. After receiving his degree as Doctor of Medicine in 1836, he continued for a time under his previous teacher, Dr. William J. Walker, who was one of the most distinguished surgeons of the time.

He next visited Europe, and spent nearly two years in the hospitals and lecture-rooms of London and Paris.

On his return he became established, in the autumn of 1838, in the city of New York, and devoted himself with ardor to the duties of his profession. He served as physician at the New York Dispensary from 1845 to 1847, and was subsequently, from 1855 to 1861, one of its trustees. About 1850 he became one of the attending surgeons of the Bellevue Hospital. This post he filled for seven years, and then felt bound to retire on account of his increasing private practice. Commencing without any special influence or acquaintance, he won his way steadily; and as he gained patients, his personal qualities made them friends.

Rev. Dr. Henry W. Bellows says of him: —

"Few men were more affectionate in disposition, and took a livelier interest in those committed to their professional care. His cordial smile in the sick-room was a medicine in itself. . . . I have seldom known a man who had more genuine confidence in the safety and value of truth. . . . Perhaps he would have risen to a more positive exceptional eminence, if he had not always been somewhat independent in his circumstances, or had possessed a more selfish and exacting ambition. But he was not clamorous for honor. . . . He belonged to the highest grade of the pure physician, and it is to be doubted whether Dr. Stone had many superiors in that class."

In our civil war Dr. Stone went several times, with other surgeons, to aid the suffering after the great battles in Pennsylvania, Maryland, and Virginia, and while in charge of the wounded Confederates at Williamsburg and Yorktown they became so attached to him as to beg him to remain permanently.

He was one of the earliest members of a society formed for the relief of widows and orphans of medical men. After serving it in various capacities for many years, he was elected its President from 1872 to 1874.

When the Metropolitan Board of Health was established in New York, Dr. Stone was appointed one of the Commissioners. He held the office during the whole existence of the Board, which was four years, from 1866 to 1869 inclusive. The reputation of this organization for effective and non-partisan work is well established, and no small part of its success may be attributed to the energy of Dr. Stone.

Dr. J. H. Emerson, Dr. Stone's medical partner, says of him in this office: —

"His sturdy integrity, shrewd common sense, great executive ability, and directness of purpose, materially aided his able coadjutors in establishing the new Board in the good opinion of the medical profession and the public. He inspired the greatest confidence in the young medical men who were selected as Health Inspectors, for they quickly found that merit, and no meretricious service, was the only way to secure his friendship and support."

One of his colleagues on the Board, Dr. James Crane of Brooklyn, thus writes: —

"There was something about him which at once secured confidence. His large, well-shaped head, and broad, overhanging brow, his plain and unpretending outward appearance, his somewhat austere and self-reliant manner, all gave assurance of the vigor and breadth of his latent powers. He was an honest man, and his integrity was unflinching and unspotted. Amply liberal and conciliatory in his differences with the opinions of others, he held to his own convictions with unyielding adherence. In our frequent deliberations the question of mere policy never seemed to arise in his mind, but right and truth had to be the absolute conditions of all procedures. This was his eminent characteristic."

Dr. Stone always took an interest in his Alma Mater, and gave heartily to its needs. In 1868 he was chosen President of the Harvard Club of New York, and served a year in that capacity. The following note in this connection speaks for itself. It is to the Secretary, under date of August 16, 1864. "Let me have three copies of the Harvard Necrology. These will be more than enough for me during these times, when every cent should be spent to assist the government or encourage the soldiers."

On June 7, 1876, Dr. Stone saw his patients, and appeared as usual, but about noon, whilst crossing Broadway near Liberty Street, he suddenly fell, and expired immediately, from disease of the heart, — a death which he had expected.

His biographer[1] thus sums up his life and character, in a passage which finds its echo in many hearts: —

"The story of his life is one unbroken record of honest and intelligent usefulness; of absolute loyalty to every duty; of great kindness in the sturdy maintenance of his own ideas of justice and truth."

In December, 1848, Dr. Stone married Catherine C., daughter of the late Patrick T. Jackson, an eminent merchant of Boston. They had five children, viz. Annie, Ellen J., Robert, Sarah J., and John. Both sons died: John in 1860, when an infant; Robert in 1867, when nearly fifteen years of age. The youngest daughter, Sarah, married, October 22, 1881, Mr. Edwin Morgan Grinnell of New York. They have one child, a daughter, born December 9, 1882.

[1] Dr. John C. Peters, who prepared a memoir of Dr. Stone for the New York Academy of Medicine, to which the Secretary has been much indebted in preparing this sketch.

JOSIAH RUTTER.

JOSIAH RUTTER, son of Micah Maynard and Nancy (Plympton) Rutter, was born at East Sudbury, now Wayland, Mass., March 2, 1813. His father, a farmer by occupation, was Major-General of militia, Deputy Sheriff, and for several years State Senator. He was fitted for college at the Framingham and Stow Academies, and entered as Freshman in 1829. As an undergraduate he was unexceptionable in conduct, but took no rank as a scholar. Modest and retiring, he did not show the talent and character he afterwards manifested. Through the four years of college life he was the chum of Charles Draper, who came from the same section of the State, and "Rutter and Draper" have a very familiar sound to the Class.

After leaving college he had charge of the Waltham High School, and afterwards kept a private school in Brighton. He then studied law in Wayland with Judge Mellen, and at the same time taught the languages in the High School of that town.

Having been admitted to the bar in Middlesex County, he established himself as a lawyer in Waltham, in July, 1843. A few years after, January 11, 1848, he married Abby E. Baldwin. He died September 3, 1876, of apoplexy, at the age of sixty-three years and six months, leaving four sons: William Baldwin, born November 9, 1848; Frederic Plympton, born August 16, 1851; Frank Josiah, born September 8, 1854; and Nathaniel Plympton, born July 25, 1857. Of these the second and third sons are married, and the former has issue.

From the notices of his death published in the Waltham papers the following extracts are made.

"A near neighbor" writes: "He was widely known and

universally respected among the members of the bar, and every client he defended was a firm friend for life. He was the first to receive the appointment of Trial Justice in this section, and held the position for about fifteen years, resigning about two years since. Though of late years he has taken but little active part in political and town affairs, in times gone by he was prominently identified with town and public interests. He represented the town in the legislature for one term, and for a period covering at least fifteen years was a member of the Board of Selectmen, and was Chairman of the Board during the largest portion of his term of service. For an equal term he was Chairman of the School Board; and hundreds of the young of both sexes would testify to his faithful and assiduous efforts for the educational interests of the town. For many years he was a Director of the Waltham Bank. On the Fourth of July last he delivered the Centennial Oration on the Common. Mr. Rutter was a gentleman of culture and scholarly attainments. His writings were models of conciseness, and he expressed his thought in the choicest words of the English language. When moved by the death of a friend, his writings were exceptionally eloquent, and no more touching and expressive words were spoken in memory of the lamented Sumner than those to which he gave utterance. He was courteous in his manner, retiring in his disposition, and honorable in all his dealings."

The following is from an editorial in the Waltham Free Press: —

"There is no better or more lasting monument to a man's memory than that reverence and respect he has awakened among the more lowly. It was the fortune of but few men who have mingled to any extent in public affairs to become so popular among the laboring classes as did Mr. Rutter, and there were always many willing to do a favor for the 'Squire,' as he was familiarly called. The position of Trial Justice, which he held for so many years, is one a man would not seek, if he would be popular with the masses; and yet few persons had a smaller number of enemies. His manner of conducting a legal suit was always satisfactory to his clients, and it is said that the hundreds he has defended were stanch friends for life."

A few days after his death the Waltham Sentinel republished a poem of Mr. Rutter's, entitled "Crazy Loker," which was written for that paper twelve years before. This, occupying nearly two columns of the paper, well sustains the opinion of "a near neighbor" by the conciseness of the narration, and by the ease and harmony of the verse.

DAVID STODDARD GREENOUGH.

DAVID STODDARD GREENOUGH was born in the old Greenough mansion at Jamaica Plain, Roxbury, Mass., July 10, 1814. His father (H. C. 1805) and grandfather were of the same name. His mother, Maria F. Doane, was the only daughter of Elijah Doane, of Cohasset (H. C. 1781). His father practised law, and might have attained eminence in his profession had he felt the stimulus of necessity. He died in 1830, when his son was in his Sophomore year.

In college our classmate took respectable rank as a scholar, and had at Commencement when we graduated a part entitled, "A Conference. 'Common Sense, Genius, and Learning. Their Characteristics, Comparative Value, and Success.'" His companions were George Inglis Crafts, of South Carolina, and Fletcher Webster. His name occurring between the other two denotes that it was "Genius" whose cause he was assigned to espouse. He was an officer in the Harvard Washington Corps, and had the Class Poem at graduating. On leaving college, he studied law, and took the degree of LL. B. in 1836. He then opened an office in Boston, but did not practise, preferring the care of his property to the assiduous toil of a young lawyer. He was for some years Colonel of the Independent Corps of Cadets, as his father had been before him. His health began to fail early. The last ten years of his life were spent in the sick-chamber, lame (from a broken hip-joint), stone deaf, and every organ except his brain partially paralyzed. He bore all these ills with a rare stoicism, retaining ever his quickness of apprehension and wit. In spite of his infirmities, he could hardly be said to be life-weary at any time. He died suddenly, of pneumonia, March 30, 1877.

He married, on the 10th of October, 1843, Anna A., daughter of the late John Parkman, of Brighton, Mass. They had five children, — four sons and one daughter. Three of the former survived him: David Stoddard, born July 16, 1844; John, born March 25, 1846; Arthur Temple, born December 3, 1857. They are all in business pursuits and prosperous. The eldest and second son (H. C. 1865) are married. The former has a son.

GEORGE EATON.

GEORGE EATON, son of Amherst and Mary (Marvin) Eaton, was born in Worcester, Mass., where his father then resided, August 19, 1812. He was fitted for college principally at the Derby Academy in Hingham. In college he roomed at No. 3 Hollis, chumming with our classmate Sydney Howard Gay, who came from the same preparatory school.

After graduating, he kept school in Stow, Mass. In 1837 he opened a school for young ladies in Springfield. He was highly esteemed as a teacher, and his school was in every way successful. He built a very expensive house, however, on a valuable lot, given him by his father, which was too much for his means. This he was forced to mortgage, and, after years of embarrassment, to part with. It proved, in short, his pecuniary ruin.

He left Springfield in 1845, and removed to Boston, where he opened a similar school in Bumstead Place.

In the years 1852 and 1853 he represented his district in the legislature. In the latter year he abandoned his school, being advised by his physician to seek some occupation less confining. But in the year 1858 he was one of the sub-masters in the Boston Latin School.

When the Webster regiment was proposed, in the spring of 1861, Eaton, who heartily sympathized with that patriotic enterprise, was placed on the Executive Committee of five, and made its Secretary. The friends of the undertaking were bent on sparing neither money nor work in making that regiment the best yet sent forth from Boston, and the office was no sinecure. This threw him into intimacy with the Webster coterie, one result of which was his ultimately becoming guardian of Ashburton, the youngest son of Fletcher Webster.

In 1862 he again represented Boston in the General Court. In 1863 he became manager of the Quincy Horse Railroad, an undertaking of which his classmate Dehon was President, and which ultimately proved unsuccessful. He lived in the town of Quincy, where he had a garden and nursery, until 1869, when he went to the city of Para, South America, for the purpose of introducing horse railroads there. He continued in that employment, which was moderately successful, until 1874. In the course of it he went four times to Brazil. His health, however, was seriously affected by the climate of South America, and he died, May 7, 1877, of Bright's disease of the kidneys, at Grantville, Mass., where his family had resided since 1869.

In 1838 he married Anne Townsend Moorfield, of Hingham, Mass., to whom he had become early attached. She was the daughter of Mr. James Moorfield, for some years a Cuban merchant. Mrs. Eaton died in the spring of 1868. They had eight children, only three of whom survived him. These are Anna Moorfield Eaton, born May 22, 1847; Charles Marion Eaton, born August 20, 1849; and Hannah Andrew Eaton, born January 22, 1852.

George Eaton was sixty-five at the time of his death. He lived a life of frequent change and excitement, — one filled with various projects, into which he entered with the ardor of a boy, but in which he soon found perseverance distasteful. He was kind and genial in his feelings, and possessed of pleasing manners. He had much general information, and was an agreeable talker. His record in the legislature was highly respectable, serving on the Committee on Education, and being placed second on the list. But the bright hopes of his early life were not fulfilled.

RICHARD SHARPE YOUNG.

RICHARD SHARPE YOUNG was the fourth son and youngest child of Alexander and Mary (Loring) Young. His father was a printer, of the firm of Young and Minns, and published the New England Palladium. He was born in Boston, February 22, 1813.

He attended the Boylston School, and afterwards went to the Latin School, in 1824. He entered college in 1829, and graduated in 1833. At Commencement he had a part, thus described in the order of performances: "A Conference. 'Contemporary and Subsequent Narrations of Historical Events.' Charles Jarvis Bates and Richard Sharpe Young."

An incident is recalled of his freshman year. During that year, some of the class, impatient that their membership in the Institute of 1770 was so long deferred, got up a new society for literary purposes. This was called the I. O. H., which at the beginning signified "Imitators of Henry," meaning the Revolutionary orator, Patrick Henry. We soon became aware of the flatness of the name, and rather ashamed of it, which indeed showed we had come to college at fourteen or fifteen instead of eighteen. How to change the name and still preserve the initials, was the puzzle. At last Young extricated us from the dilemma by suggesting the following: "Imitatores omnium honestorum." His proposition was unanimously accepted, and the society flourished for many years.

After leaving college, Young studied medicine with Dr. Walker of Charlestown, graduated at the Harvard Medical School in 1837, was a member of the Massachusetts Medical Society, and practised Medicine in Boston. He wrote often for the press over the signature of "Digby." In 1850 he went to California, where he continued the practice of his profession and his literary labors. In the midst of his work he was seized with rheumatic fever, which left him in a feeble state of health, from which he never recovered. His hands were bent and drawn together, so that he was obliged to have an attendant a great deal of the time. He died in San Francisco, August 9, 1877, aged sixty-four years and five weeks, and his body was buried in the cemetery at Mount Auburn.

The testimony of those who knew him best is that he was very kind and gentle, generous, unselfish, and that he would do more for others than for himself. He was fond of children, and played with them. He had a love for music, and possessed a good voice. A sensitive disposition, naturally shy and diffident, made him reserved, and prevented him from doing justice to his powers.

He was in full sympathy with the movement for the abolition of slavery, and was a friend of Sumner and other leaders in that struggle.

Most of the above sketch was furnished by a relative.

CHRISTOPHER MINOT WELD.

CHRISTOPHER MINOT WELD was the son of William Gordon and Hannah (Minot) Weld of Boston, and was born in that city, January 19, 1812. He went some time to the Latin School, but was fitted for college at the school of his brother, Stephen M. Weld, at Jamaica Plain, where he afterwards taught during his college vacations. He entered Harvard at the beginning of the sophomore year, and graduated in due course.

He studied medicine with Dr. George C. Shattuck, and became a convert to homœopathy about the year 1838. He began practice in Boston, but soon removed to Jamaica Plain. In 1839 he married Miss Marianne P. Jarvis, of Boston, sister of our classmate William P. Jarvis.

His business soon became large, and for nearly a quarter of a century he stood in his lot, spending and being spent for others. There are different opinions as to the value of his mode of practice, but there was no question in the minds of those who knew him then as to the untiring devotion and faithfulness with which he performed all the duties incident to a large practice. This was more onerous in his case because of there being no other homœopathic physician within a considerable distance. At length, the professional labors so heartily performed proved beyond his strength. His health gave way, and he was forced to relinquish practice. This occurred in 1862. He immediately went abroad, accompanied by his wife. He remained in Europe nearly four years, passing much time in England, France, and Italy, and three months in Spain. He returned with improved health, but was unable to resume practice. In 1872 he made a second visit to Europe, and remained two years. His health after his return was not good, and, though he continued to attend Commencement, he looked more and more like a confirmed invalid. His last sickness was pneumonia, and he died at Jamaica Plain, after an illness of a week, March 14, 1878

For his classmates he ever preserved a lively and affectionate remembrance, and there was none whose smiling face was more welcomed in all class gatherings. He was noted, in fact, for his fervent attachment to everything that concerned his Alma Mater, — in season and out of season her welfare was to him an agreeable theme, and he was always ready to promote it in any manner in his power.

Immediately after the death of Dr. Weld, the following announcement appeared in the Boston papers.

"BOSTON HOMŒOPATHIC MEDICAL SOCIETY. — *The Late Dr. Weld.* At the regular meeting of this Society, held at the Medical College, East Concord Street, on Thursday evening, the following resolutions were unanimously adopted: —

"Whereas, Death has removed our respected associate and beloved friend, Christopher Minot Weld, M. D., a man whose knowledge, skill, and conscientious devotion to his profession, whose upright character, gentle spirit, and warm sympathies, placed him in the rank of the true physician, and gave him a position of great influence and respect in this community; and

"Whereas, With a mind receptive to all truth, he, early in his professional life, now nearly forty years ago, examined homœopathy, believed in it, and though it ostracized him from many of his professional brethren, and subjected him to obloquy and harsh criticism, yet with a high sense of duty adopted it; and

"Whereas, For a quarter-century, until failing health compelled him to relinquish active practice, in a very extensive circle of patients, he exhibited its curative power and beneficent results, and up to his latest moments maintained an unswerving belief in its truth, and sought to add to its practical importance, therefore, —

"*Resolved*, That we cordially testify our respect for one so noble and so good, who sacrificed so much for the welfare of others, and who accomplished so much for his profession and for humanity.

"*Resolved*, That we invite the physicians of Massachusetts to unite with us in the last sad obsequies to our departed brother."

ANDREW FOSTER.

ANDREW FOSTER, eldest son of Andrew and Mary (Conant) Foster, was born January 5, 1815. His father (H. C. 1800) was established as a physician successively in Dedham, Roxbury, and Cambridge, Mass. His parents were married in Cambridge, November 19, 1813, and his father died in that town in 1831.

Foster took no rank in his class, but went through the prescribed course, and graduated in 1833.

Very little is known of his life for the first twenty-five years after leaving college. There seems to have been a peculiar mortality among his early friends and companions; even his three brothers, all younger than himself, having died before him. It is thought that he pursued the study of the law for a while. He is believed, again, to have been attached to the editorial staff of some Boston newspaper. About ten years after graduating, at the death of the widow of his only maternal grand-uncle, Mr. Andrew Craigie, who owned and occupied the fine old mansion in Cambridge so well known subsequently as the home of Longfellow, he inherited with his three brothers that house, and the extensive fields adjoining, now covered with scores of pleasant homes.

September 16, 1849, whilst living at Lawrence, Mass., he married Delia, widow of his brother, James Foster, U. S. N.

At our twenty-fifth anniversary, in 1858, he was set down on the "Roll Call" as of New York, and a merchant. This is doubtless correct. He was probably then in the iron trade there, with his brother George, who owned an iron foundry.

Before leaving Massachusetts, he was for a time a stockbroker in Boston. On moving to New York, he resumed that vocation, either before his experience as an iron merchant or afterwards.

About 1860 he became a sufferer from asthma, and to relieve his pains had recourse to stimulants. This grew into a habit, and greatly aggravated his complaints. His decline nevertheless was gradual; so lately as 1876 he retained enough of his old self to obtain admission into the society of "The Cincinnati," as successor of his grand-uncle, Andrew Craigie. But after this time his habits grew upon him until he was overpowered by them.

He became a Roman Catholic before his death; and, separated from family and friends, he expired, September 22, 1879, at the Kings County Hospital, Brooklyn, N. Y., and was buried in the Flatbush Cemetery.

His widow survived him; also two children, — Andrew Foster, now employed in a business position in California, and Kate McRay Foster, who at present lives with her mother in New York.

WILLIAM PORTER JARVIS.

WILLIAM PORTER JARVIS, son of Benjamin and Mary (Porter) Jarvis, was born in Boston, March 5, 1812. His father was a merchant and selectman of the town of Boston. He was fitted for college at the school of Stephen M. Weld, of Jamaica Plain. Though he graduated with the class, his name does not appear in the annual catalogue until the sophomore year. On graduating he studied law, but being fond of literary pursuits, and interested in the subject of education, he was for several years engaged in the occupation of teaching. Possessed by inheritance of a competency, and being unmarried, he gratified his taste by collecting a fine library, which he much enjoyed, and also by twice visiting Europe, — the last time joining his brother-in-law and sister, Dr. and Mrs. Weld, on their first visit abroad, and accompanying them to Spain.

Commencement was always a field day to him, and it is doubtful whether any of the class attended its services so punctually, or enjoyed them so serenely.

He died at Boston, after a protracted breaking up, of softening of the brain, May 29, 1880.

FREDERIC AUGUSTUS WHITNEY.

FREDERIC AUGUSTUS WHITNEY, son of the Rev. Peter and Jane (Lincoln) Whitney, was born in Quincy, Mass., September 13, 1812. His father, grandfather, and great-grandfather were ministers, settled nearly fifty years, and until death, over the First Congregational Church at Quincy, Northborough, and Petersham, Mass., respectively.

He was fitted for college by his father, and graduated with honor, in 1833. While a student in Harvard College, he was also mathematical tutor in the noted classical school of Mr. William Wells at Cambridge. On graduating, he was employed by Mr. Stephen M. Weld in his equally noted school at Jamaica Plain.

Having chosen the family profession, he went through the Divinity School at Cambridge, and graduated there in 1838. He was first employed by the American Unitarian Association, in missionary work in Massachusetts and at the South and West. In April, 1843, he was invited to take charge of the First Congregational Church at Brighton, Mass. He accepted the invitation, and remained pastor of the church for sixteen years.

January 11, 1853, he married Elizabeth Perkins, daughter of the late William Perkins and Joanna (Stetson) Matchett, of Boston. They had no children.

Resigning his parochial office in 1859, he continued for more than twenty years to live in Brighton, — the circumstances of his wife allowing him to dispense with a salary. He had made himself during his active ministry much respected and beloved in the parish, and until the end of life he was frequently called on for parochial services. Nor were his public labors confined to his old parish, — the whole town came to appreciate his faithfulness and persevering industry. He published, in this connection, thirteen annual reports as chairman of the School Committee, nine annual reports as President of the Board of Trustees of the Public Library, and the large catalogue of the books therein, — the labor on this last being undertaken with insufficient help, and being prosecuted early and late.

Besides the several town reports, and sermons on various occasions, Mr. Whitney published the following: —

An Historical Sketch of the Old Church at Quincy, Mass.
Biographical Sketches of Josiah Quincy, Jr. and John Hancock.

Biography of James Holton, Founder of the Holton Library (from which grew the Brighton Public Library).

Oration at the Dedication of the Soldiers' Monument, with an Historical Appendix.

Address at the Consecration of Evergreen Cemetery, with an Historical Appendix.

Just before he was seized with his last sickness, he had completed the History of Brighton, comprising one chapter in Samuel Adams Drake's History of Middlesex County, Mass.

In enumerating his writings, the diary he kept should not be forgotten. This was begun, January 1, 1827, two years and a half before he went to college, and continued to January 18, 1880, when illness compelled him to give it up, — a period of fifty-three years. This has been more than once referred to as an arbiter of doubtful points. It will remain of value, and ought to be carefully preserved.

In a volume entitled "Singers and Songs of the Liberal Faith," prepared by the Rev. Alfred P. Putnam, of Brooklyn, N. Y., in which several occasional hymns by Mr. Whitney were inserted, is found a brief biography. In this, Mr. Putnam speaks of all these biographies, genealogies, sketches, catalogues, and reports, as giving evidence of conscientious and painstaking care in their preparation, as showing a habit of patient research, and altogether forming a valuable contribution to the department of literature to which they belong.

He died of disease of the brain, at his house in Gardner Street, Brighton, October 21, 1880, having been ill about nine months. He was buried on Monday, October 25, from his own church, Rev. Dr. A. P. Peabody, Plummer Professor at Harvard, delivering a commemorative address. Though Monday is at Brighton the busiest day of the week, yet the church was filled. The following classmates acted as pallbearers: Francis Bowen, Joseph Lovering, H. W. Torrey, George E. Ellis, and Morrill Wyman.

RUFUS CAMPBELL TORREY.

RUFUS C. TORREY, very thoughtfully, as if with a premonition that he should not live to the Commencement of 1883, sent to Professor Bowen, in 1882, the following brief autobiography.

"Rufus Campbell Torrey, son of John and Sally (Richardson) Torrey, was born at Oxford, Mass., February 13, 1813. His parents having died while he was quite young, he was removed to Franklin under the charge of a maternal uncle. He pursued his preparatory studies at the Academy in Wrentham, and entered Harvard College as a freshman in August, 1829. He graduated in due course, in August, 1833. His rank as a scholar placed him near the middle of a class of fifty-five. After leaving college he spent three or four years in Fitchburg, engaged mostly in teaching and editing a newspaper. He also wrote a history of the town of Fitchburg, — a volume of about 130 pages, — which was reprinted in 1865.

Near the close of the year 1838 he removed to Mobile, and for two years was engaged in teaching, and studying law under the supervision of Judge B. T. Harris, and was admitted to the bar at the close of the year 1840. In 1841 he commenced the practice of his profession at Grove Hill, Ala., and removed thence to Claiborne in 1843, where he has continued to reside to the present time.

In 1844 he was elected Judge of the County Court of Monroe County, which office comprised those of Judge of Probate and presiding Judge of the Court of County Commissioners. This office he resigned after a tenure of four years. For twenty-five years he was an active member of the Masonic Fraternity, and was elected Grand Master of the R. and S. Masters of the State. He led a quiet and uneventful life till 1875, when he was elected a member of the convention called to revise the Constitution of the State. In 1876 he was chosen a State Senator for the term of four years. He was married, in 1846, to Elizabeth, only daughter of the late Andrew Henshaw. Four children were the issue of this marriage, three of whom, two sons and a daughter, have reached their majority, and are residing in Mobile.

Deafness and other infirmities increasing with advancing age induced Mr. Torrey to retire from the practice of the law in 1879. He was in comfortable circumstances at the beginning of the late civil war, but the results of that unhappy misunderstanding reduced him, as they have thousands of others, to comparative poverty."

Rufus C. Torrey died at Claiborne, Ala., September 13, 1882, of the pulmonary disease from which he had so long suffered. He was in the active practice of his profession to within a few years of his death, thus showing the wisdom of his emigration, forty-four years ago, to the mild climate of Alabama.

The Mobile Daily Register, a few days after his death, speaks of him as one of the most estimable men in South Alabama, and as one who left his impress on the people and institutions of the State. The concluding paragraph of its notice is here given, to which those who can recall the amiable traits of our classmate will readily respond.

"He was of a firm yet gentle disposition, supremely upright in all his transactions, and eminently just to all men, — a man noted for his constant observance of the Golden Rule, — a man who died leaving not one enemy. In the counties of Clarke and Monroe, where his example shone the brightest, among his near neighbors and life-long friends, where he married and toiled, and whence he but Wednesday passed away, his loss will be deeply felt."

JOHN CHESTER LYMAN.

THE Secretary has received the following from a near friend of Mr. Lyman.

"He was born in Northampton, Mass., August 8, 1813. He was the son of Jonathan H. Lyman, a prominent lawyer in his day. He prepared for college at Canandaigua Academy and at Round Hill School, Northampton, and went through the collegiate course at Harvard. Afterwards he spent three years abroad. Returning, he entered the Harvard Law School, and, on graduating, opened an office in Boston, but remained in the profession only a short time, being sent by his grandfather, Judge Hinckley, to South America on business. He never resumed his practice, but, having means independent of his profession, spent much of his time in reading, in society, and in travel.

"He married, in 1854, Mary, daughter of Hon. Mathias Morris, of Doylestown, Pa. Since his marriage, he has resided chiefly in that place. His health has always been more or less delicate, which has been in great measure the reason of his not leading a more active life. He has two sons and two daughters."

The above was written in September, 1882. From accounts of Lyman's health received at the same time, the announcement of his death, six months after, occasioned little surprise. It occurred on February 27, 1883. From a letter received from Mrs. Lyman, dated March 9, 1883, the following extract is made: —

"Mr. Lyman's death was caused by exhaustion, rather than disease. It was a general breaking up of the system. His health had been decidedly declining for a year or two, and he finally passed away peacefully and painlessly."

Of the four children, the eldest son, Richard Morris, will be twenty-four next October. He is a lawyer, and was admitted to the bar last November. The youngest son, Robert Huntington, is sixteen. The ages of the two daughters are between the above.

The Bucks County Intelligencer of March 3, 1883, contains the following obituary.

"DEATH OF JOHN C. LYMAN.

"John Chester Lyman, one of our oldest citizens, died at his home, corner of Broad and Main Streets, Doylestown, last Tuesday evening, about half-past nine o'clock, in the sixty-ninth year of his age."

After reciting the early events of his life as given above, the notice goes on: —

"He had some experience at the Boston Bar in certain patent cases; but his literary tastes and love for travel soon induced him to go abroad, and he made several trips to Europe, one to South America, and also travelled a good deal in this country.

"It was during one of his trips across the Atlantic that he became acquainted with Miss Mary Ann Morris, daughter of the Hon. Mathias Morris, who represented this Congressional District in the Twenty-fourth Congress, and a niece of the Hon. Henry Chapman. He subsequently married Miss Morris, and, after living a short time in Philadelphia, came to Doylestown about the year 1858, where he has lived ever since.

"Mr. Lyman has resided here as a private citizen, never holding public office, and never engaging in active business. He was a vestryman of St. Paul's Episcopal Church for a number of years before his death. He had a large circle of friends, and those who were on intimate terms with him admired his brilliant talents and his well-stored mind. He was a constant reader almost to the day of his death. He had the reputation of doing many kind acts, in a quiet way, among his neighbors, especially among those who were poor."

NOTICES OF THE SURVIVORS.

NOTICES OF THE SURVIVORS.

SAMUEL PAGE ANDREWS.

SALEM, May 3, 1882.

MY DEAR MR. HIGGINSON,—I don't suppose it would be safe to address a President in any less formal way than that, or I should have said, My dear Waldo. Here's the life of Samuel Page Andrews. Born at Salem in the cold winter, (and he has never got over the chill of that inclement season,) December 8, 1813. Carried in his tender infancy up to Danvers to preserve his precious life from the ferocious British, who were continually threatening his native place; returned with the return of peace to his home, placed in one of the old and many-gabled houses of the town at the age of four, under the care of Marm Oliver,—an ancient dame of the very old school, fat and easy, whose chief employment and duty were to take snuff and sleep, while the youngsters under her care were engaged in the serious work of education; to wit, skylarking, and catching handfuls of flies and letting them off under her nose, to the great disturbance of her needed and well-merited repose. I think this good old lady—good in descent, good to her scholars, and very good to herself—was nearly eighty years of age when she took charge of his education. From her, after a year's discipline, he was transferred to Marm Bowditch, a young and flighty dame of not more than seventy years, of whom his recollections are not so vivid as of his first teacher; from her, at the age of six or seven, transferred to Marm Leach, a still younger dame of thirty-five or forty, of severe countenance, who ruled from her throne her boys with a rod of birch, and at whose head he found it necessary (on the day of his instalment) to throw his primer for some fancied injustice; placed at the ripe age of eight under care of John Walsh (son of Walsh's Arithmetic), where, in company with Ben Peirce, Ingersoll Bowditch, and he thinks Nat also, and a lot of other youngsters and oldsters, most of whom have gone up, he was inducted into the mysteries of Latin grammar and of that same arithmetic of blessed memory.

After some three years' fighting with the boys of the Public Latin School, he was removed to that school, where, under the sharp discipline of Theo Eames and the somewhat milder rule of Henry K. Oliver (who still survives, and whose joke it is to say that he went to school with me, making himself, with his more than eighty years of age, a contemporary), he was fitted for college, — if being crammed with the Latin and Greek Grammars, and all their rules and exceptions, can be called fitting. In college he did n't do much, except have a reasonably good time, and he is satisfied that, if the thing were to be gone over with again, he could neither get into college nor out of it. Instead of devoting himself to the curriculum of the Old Dame, whom in after years we call the "Dear Mother," he spent no inconsiderable part of his time in roving about the country with dear old Jeffries Wyman (of more than blessed memory), dissecting snakes and frogs and cats and dogs, and picking up heaps of stones which were dignified with the name of minerals. These dissections and the stones having taught him the vanity of earthly things, he entered the Divinity School to see if anything substantial could be found there, though with no very strong intention of pursuing the profession for which the studies at that place were supposed to be a preparation. After preaching about and about for a year, his health broke down and he dawdled, loafed, for two years, when he went into business in Boston, hoping to make money enough to buy a farm, the living upon which had been, in the phrase of these days, "the dream of his life." He did n't make the money, but bought the farm all the same, — a small farm in Framingham, — having in the mean time married Rebecca Bacon Scudder, born in Boston, July 4, 1818, but at the time of her marriage living in Barnstable. This was on October 15, 1845. Here, i. e. in Framingham, he remained for a while, and after seven years of hard but extremely pleasant and congenial work he returned to his old home in Salem, — the health of his wife requiring a change, and his two children, Abby Bacon, born August 5, 1846, and William Page,[1] born November 22, 1848, needing some better or more convenient educational advantages than could be readily obtained in Framingham. Here he stayed for a year doing nothing; but finding this to be hard work, he accepted the position of Clerk of the Police Court in Salem, and afterwards of the First District Court of Essex, to which he was appointed by the Governor in June, 1874. And here he has been all these years, and has seen enough of misery and misfortune in others, and of wrong-doing and suffering, to satisfy any reasonable person, and to furnish the groundwork of ten thousand dime novels.

You wanted his life, (I don't mean criminally,) and you have it. If you had thought he was going to last so long, you probably would n't have asked for it. Make the best or the worst of it that you can. "Drop a tear" over its misfortune, and rejoice over what of success it may have had. If it should last till the fiftieth anniversary, the holder of it will hope to meet the surviving remnants, — the "rari nantes." Must have some Latin for the credit of the class (even if it is n't good grammar) of 1833.

Yours most truly,
SAMUEL P. ANDREWS.

[1] See note, page 143.

JAMES LORING BAKER.

JAMES L. BAKER, after graduating, studied law. Being admitted to the Suffolk Bar, he opened an office in Boston. He soon abandoned the law to go into the manufacturing business of his father at Hingham, Mass., in which he continued some years. After giving it up, he continued to reside in Hingham.

He was a frequent contributor to newspapers, and his papers, printed in the Boston Transcript, were collected and published in a handsome volume under the title of "Men and Things."

In 1875 he removed to Minneapolis, Minn., where he now resides.

He has been twice married: — 1st. May 9, 1850, to Nancy R., daughter of Hon. Zabdiel Sampson, of Plymouth, Mass. She died, May 9, 1854. 2d. May 5, 1860, to Susan F. Lunenburg, of Boston. He has had one son and three daughters by his second wife, and two of his daughters are now living.

FRANCIS BOWEN.

THE following notice is mainly from "The Harvard Book," published in 1874, with some additions and amendments furnished by Professor Bowen.

Francis Bowen, born in Charlestown, Mass., September 8, 1811, received his early education at the Mayhew Grammar School, in Boston. For a few years he was junior clerk in a publishing office in Boston; in January, 1829, he became a pupil in Phillips Exeter Academy, and in August, 1830, he entered the sophomore class in Harvard College. In the winter of 1829–30, he taught school at Hampton Falls, N. H.; and in the three following winters, successively, at Lexington, Northborough, and Concord, Mass. Graduating at Harvard with the first honors of his class in 1833, he became instructor in mathematics in Phillips Exeter Academy, and continued to act in that capacity till August, 1835. He then returned to Harvard, where he was first made Tutor in Greek, and, a year afterwards, was appointed instructor of the senior class in mental philosophy and political economy. This office he held for three years, being much occupied also with literary pursuits. In 1837 he contributed to Sparks's "Library of American Biography" a Life of Sir William Phipps; and he afterwards furnished for the same work Lives of James Otis, Baron Steuben, and Benjamin Lincoln. He was also a frequent contributor to the literary periodicals of that day. In August, 1839, he resigned his office in the College, and went to Europe, where he spent a year in study and travel.

On his return, he established his residence in Cambridge, and devoted himself for the next twelve years to literature as a profession. In 1842 appeared his edition of Virgil, with English notes and a considerable amount of illustrative and critical matter. At that period comparatively few American editions of the classics had appeared; and this work, though never revised or purged of numerous errors and defects, has been kept in the market by successive issues from the same stereotype plates, and is still in considerable use. In the same year he published a volume of "Critical Essays on Speculative Philosophy," devoted chiefly to the systems of Kant, Fichte, and Cousin, and to the evidences of Christianity as affected by the developments of metaphysical doctrines.

In 1843 Mr. Bowen became the owner and editor of "The North American Review," and continued to conduct this work for the next eleven years. He also edited and published, for six years, "The American Almanac and Repository of Useful Knowledge." In 1849 he published, in an octavo volume, two courses of "Lowell Lectures on the Application of Metaphysical and Ethical Science to the Evidences of Religion." Six years afterwards, this work, revised and enlarged, appeared in a second edition, and continued in use for a considerable time as a text-book at Harvard.

In 1850 Mr. Bowen was appointed by the Corporation to the McLean Professorship of History in the College, but held this office only six months. In 1853 he was nominated and confirmed as Alford Professor of Natural Religion, Moral Philosophy, and Civil Polity, and still continues to act under this appointment. In 1879 he received from Harvard College, with his classmates Professors Lovering and Torrey, the degree of LL. D.

Besides those already mentioned, he has published the following works: —

Behr's Translation of Weber's Outlines of Universal History, revised and corrected, with the Addition of a History of the United States. 1853.

Dugald Stewart's Philosophy of the Human Mind, revised and abridged, with Critical and Explanatory Notes. 1854.

Documents of the Constitution of England and America, from Magna Charta to the Federal Constitution of 1789, compiled and edited, with Notes. 1854.

The Principles of Political Economy applied to the Condition and Institutions of the American People. 1856.

The Metaphysics of Sir William Hamilton, collected, arranged, and abridged, for the Use of Colleges and Private Students. 1862.

De Tocqueville's Democracy in America, edited with Notes, the Translation revised, and in great part rewritten, and the Additions made to the recent Paris Editions now first translated. 1862.

A Treatise on Logic, or the Laws of Pure Thought, comprising both the Aristotelic and Hamiltonian Analyses of Logical Forms, and some Chapters of Applied Logic. 1864.

American Political Economy, including Strictures on the Management of the Currency and the Conduct of the Finances since 1861. New York, 1870.
Modern Philosophy, from Descartes to Schopenhauer and Hartmann. New York, 1877.
Gleanings from a Literary Life, 1838–1880. New York, 1880.

Professor Bowen served on the U. S. Silver Commission in 1876. His colleagues were Senators Boutwell, Jones of Nevada, and Bogy of Missouri; Representatives Bland, Gibson, and Willard; Expert, W. S. Groesbeck.

Professor Bowen married, November 1, 1848, Arabella Stuart, daughter of Charles Stuart, Esq., of Lancaster, N. H., and niece of Rev. Daniel Austin. His only son, Charles Stuart Bowen, was born in July, 1850, and graduated at Harvard in 1871. He has two daughters surviving, the elder, Maria, the younger, Helen Elizabeth. All three children live at home, unmarried.

LUTHER CLARK.

DR. CLARK has sent to the secretary the following particulars.

"Studied medicine, and after taking his degree as M. D. in 1836, commenced practice in Boston, where he has since mostly resided. He has been a member of the Massachusetts Medical Society since joining it in 1836.

In 1840 he adopted the principles and practice of homœopathy, to which he has since adhered, though strongly opposed to the absurd infinitesimals which have brought such discredit upon the system and such wrong to patients in need of medicine.

In 1843 he married Selina Cranch Minot, of Boston. Has

had five children, of whom a son, Theodore M. (H. C. 1866), architect, and a daughter (Mrs. Geo. Ropes), survive.

For some years past he has been in poor health; has now relinquished practice, and resides a part of the time at the South."

GEORGE INGLIS CRAFTS.

THE secretary received the following from Mr. Crafts under dates of Charleston, S. C., July 11 and November 27, 1882.

I was born in 1812 or '13; then Charleston College to senior year. After graduating at Cambridge returned to Charleston. Studied or tried to study law; was " admitted to the bar" in '35 or '36: never got much practice or reputation, and less money. In 1846 went off for a European tour; took two years on it, — Palestine and the Nile to the Cataracts, then Greece and Spain, having done Italy and Switzerland previously. Returning to Charleston end of '47, instead of trying law again, as I ought to have done, undertook the cultivation of a small plantation near here, which had been in my family a long time, and which furnished the means of living very economically without too much mental exertion. The summer of 1853 went over to France in charge of a sick cousin; passed it quietly with Prince Lucien Murat, near Paris, who had married, when living in New Jersey, a cousin of mine, and who, on accession of the Bonapartes to power, removed with his family to France. In the next two years I lived here quietly, attending to my farm business. March, 1855, was married to Miss Mary Anderson of Florida and New York; then made a third trip across the water, returning here and living on very quietly and comfortably until the war broke out in '60. Having received a commission as Captain in Quartermaster's Department, was stationed here and served to the end.

Mrs. Crafts died in April, 1865,[1] leaving me with two daughters, now twenty-four and twenty-one, unmarried, and one son, William,[2] now about nineteen.

Since end of war I have been living here continuously, we having a *small* income from property of Mrs. C. in New York.

As regards my bodily health, I keep perfectly sound, nothing but a few headaches ever troubling me, but I weigh only a little more than one hundred pounds.

Always yours faithfully,
G. I. CRAFTS.

HIRAM KEITH CURTIS.

HIRAM KEITH CURTIS, after graduating, adopted the profession of a civil engineer. He entered the office of Colonel Loammi Baldwin at Charlestown, Mass., then esteemed the best school in that art. He remained there a number of years, and was much valued for his skill and thoroughness. About ten years after leaving college, whilst shooting, he met with an accident, by which he lost one eye and one hand, — a very serious loss in his chosen profession.

The above sketch was sent to Curtis, June 2, 1882. He soon returned it, with the following conclusion.

---

[1] Her death made one of the many sad tragedies of the war. After the occupation of Columbia, S. C., by General Sherman, Mrs. Crafts — being separated from her husband, who was obliged to leave her there, and misled by false rumors — set out, with her three young children, to reach New York, where she had relatives. She succeeded in doing so, after exposures and privations lasting many weeks; but these hardships cost her life. She arrived in New York only to die.

[2] Now a student in the Massachusetts Institute of Technology.

"After lying by for repairs a year and a half, he gradually began work again, and about five years afterwards retired to East Stoughton and has lain dormant there ever since."

In a note accompanying the return he says: "Though quiet and useless, I would not have you think me disappointed or morose. I feel that I have had more than a fair chance in the world."

JOHN HOMER DIX.

MR. HIGGINSON: —

DEAR SIR, — September 9, 1840, I performed the first operation for strabismus, or cross-eye, on this side of the Atlantic. On the following day it was performed at Pittsfield, by Dr. Willard Parker, of New York.

Soon after, I announced in the Boston Medical and Surgical Journal my withdrawal from general practice, and that I should treat only diseases of the eye and ear. This step was regarded unfavorably by my best professional friends, and, so far as I know, was the earliest instance of a man of regular standing in this country adopting an exclusive specialty and adhering to it. In my old age, it is a great satisfaction to me that so many men of large intelligence and thorough education have taken the same course.

In 1849 I obtained a Boylston prize for an Essay on Morbid Sensibility of the Retina. It was published, and is, I believe, the first work to give what is now generally accepted as the *rationale* of the disease. It is now admitted that the term above used was a misnomer, and the disease is now called Asthenopia.

In 1857, against the remonstrance of friends, I began to build the Hotel Pelham, of which Mr. King, in the Handbook of Boston, says that "it was the first building of the French flats or family hotel class, and that this mode of habitation gained its foothold in America by its introduction here."

Five years elapsed before a building for this purpose was erected in New York. They are now counted by hundreds in Boston, and by thousands in New York.

This is all I recall creditable to myself and of interest to others, and if you feel disposed to wonder at the length of the statement, remember that you brought it on yourself, and that you are spared the much longer list of faults and failures. These last I am striving to forget, but if you care to know them, ask my relatives, friends, and patients.

Yours truly,
J. H. DIX.

June 27, 1882.

Dr. Dix married, June 9, 1858, Helen Pelham, daughter of the late Thomas Curtis and half-sister to the late Charles P. and Thomas B. Curtis, all three well-known Bostonians.

CHARLES DRAPER.

PONTIAC, MICH., June 8, 1882.

MR. HIGGINSON: —

DEAR SIR, — The year of my graduation I left Massachusetts, and came to Michigan; my place of residence has ever since been at Pontiac. My father, William Draper, was a graduate at Harvard, and he removed to this place from Marlborough about six months before the time I did.

Early after arriving here I taught an academy for a short time, — Pontiac was then a frontier town. I taught the first academic school in Northern Michigan.

I studied law in the office of my father for several years, and was admitted to practise in 1840.

The pleasantest part of my life was the first years of my residence in Michigan. All things were new and fresh, — the inhabitants, their habits, customs, and manner of living. Society was in no wise hampered by conventionalities. I became a married man in 1840. I have three sons and one daughter. The three sons are lawyers by profession; and in the providence of God I have been greatly favored, — all my children are still living.

Michigan was admitted into the Union as a State in 1836, and for twenty years was a strong Democratic State. Soon after the adoption of the State Constitution I was elected County Clerk of Oakland County, and held that office for several years: was subsequently elected for several terms to the office of Prosecuting Attorney of the same county, and in 1867 was chosen State Senator, and finally, so far as office-holding is concerned, was appointed United States Assessor, and then Register in Bankruptcy. You can gather from this that I have been a Republican, and wish it understood I am still such, and in all human probability shall die in that political faith.

Affectionately your friend and classmate,

CHARLES DRAPER.

In a letter received by the secretary under date of April 10, 1883, Draper says: "As for myself, my strength both physical and mental holds out remarkably. Can read and write without the use of spectacles, and with eye and hand as clear and steady as on the day I graduated from Old Harvard, — God bless her. My step is as strong and firm as it then was."

GEORGE EDWARD ELLIS.

GEORGE EDWARD ELLIS, son of David and Sarah (Rogers) Ellis, was born in Boston, August 8, 1814.

He was fitted for college at the Boston Latin School, Round Hill School, Northampton, and the school of Mr. William Wells, Cambridge. He entered Harvard College in 1829, and graduated in 1833.

Choosing the profession of a clergyman, he entered the Theological School at Cambridge, and completed its course of study in 1836.

Soon after leaving Cambridge he visited Europe. On his return, he preached at various churches in Boston and its vicinity, with great acceptance; and the Harvard Church in Charlestown, which Rev. Dr. James Walker had recently left, invited him to become their minister. He accepted their offer, and was ordained on March 11, 1840.

In 1857, Mr. Ellis was chosen Professor of Systematic Theology in the Divinity School at Cambridge. Residence not being required, he accepted this office, and performed its duties until 1863. In 1857, also, the degree of Doctor of Divinity was conferred upon him by Harvard College.

In 1869, after an incumbency of nearly thirty years, he resigned his pastorate at Charlestown, to take effect on the 1st of July in that year.

Since that date, he has preferred to remain without parochial cares, and to devote himself chiefly to literary labors.

On the 15th of April, 1840, about a month after his ordination, Mr. Ellis married Elizabeth Bruce, daughter of Mr. William Eager, of Boston. Mrs. Ellis died, April 10, 1842, leaving one son, John Harvard Ellis, born in Charlestown, January 9. 1841. This son graduated at Harvard in 1862, took his degree of LL. B. in 1864, was admitted to the

Boston Bar, and contributed some articles to the American Law Review. In 1867 he edited a sumptuous edition of the works of Anne Bradstreet in prose and verse. On the 25th of March, 1869, he married Grace Atkinson, daughter of Mr. James L. Little. Up to this time, and somewhat later, he appeared to have as fair prospects of life and health as belong to most young men. He became ill, however, when in Europe, on his wedding tour. His malady was at first obscure; but, on his return to Boston, it soon developed itself in the form of disease of the lungs, and he died in that city, May 3, 1870, at the age of twenty-nine.

On the 22d of October, 1859, Dr. Ellis married, as his second wife, Lucretia Goddard, daughter of Mr. Benjamin Apthorp Gould (H. C. 1814), for many years head-master of the Boston Latin School. Mrs. Ellis died at Mount Desert, Maine, July 6, 1869, a few days after her husband's connection with his parish in Charlestown had been dissolved.

The events of Dr. Ellis's life not stated above — his services and honors not already mentioned — are best narrated in a passage from his biography, contained in the "History of the Harvard Church in Charlestown,"[1] to which the Secretary is already much indebted.

"During the entire period of his residence in Charlestown, Dr. Ellis took an active interest in the public schools, and in all educational matters, serving several years on the School Committee. He was no less active with his pen, having written much in the interest of education. To the New York Review, the North American Review, and the Atlantic Monthly he has been a large contributor, chiefly on topics of American history, of which he has been a close and life-long student; while he has occasionally written for the Monthly Religious Magazine. He has also contributed several articles to the ninth edition of the Encyclopædia Britannica. He

---

[1] History of the Harvard Church in Charlestown, 1815-1879. Boston: Printed for the Society. 1879. pp. 294.

was at one time the editor of the Christian Register, with the Rev. Dr. George Putnam, and subsequently alone. He also conducted the Christian Examiner for several years.

"In 1864, he delivered before the Lowell Institute a course of lectures on 'The Evidences of Christianity'; in 1871, a course on 'The Provincial History of Massachusetts'; and in 1879, a course on 'The Red Man and the White Man in North America.'

"Dr. Ellis early received the honors of the Massachusetts Historical Society, of which he is one of the most prominent members and a Vice-President. He has contributed largely to their published volumes of 'Proceedings,' and has edited several volumes of the Society's 'Collections.' He has also received the diploma of the American Academy of Arts and Sciences, of the American Antiquarian Society, and of the Historical Societies of New York and other States. From 1850 to 1854 he was a member of the Board of Overseers of Harvard College, and its Secretary, 1853-54. He withdrew his name as a candidate, when presented by the Alumni for re-election to the Board in 1879. From 1871 to 1874 he was a trustee of the Massachusetts General Hospital."

At the end of this notice of Dr. Ellis, Mr. Henry H. Edes adds what is believed to be a perfect list of his separate publications up to the time of printing the "History of the Harvard Church," in 1879. This list, together with a catalogue of his papers in several reviews and magazines, and of his contributions to the Proceedings of the Massachusetts Historical Society and of the American Antiquarian Society, fill ten pages in an octavo pamphlet.

Since 1879 the following works have been published by him : —

In Memorial History of Boston, Vol. I., 1880, chapter on "The Puritan Commonwealth," pp. 141-191 ; and chapter on "The Indians of Eastern Massachusetts," pp. 241-275. In Vol. II., 1881, chapter on "The Royal Governors," pp. 27-93.

Memoir of Jacob Bigelow, M. D., LL. D. 1880. pp. 105.
Introduction to the History of the First Church in Boston. 1881. pp. 74.
The Red Man and the White Man in North America, from its Discovery to the Present Time. 1882. pp. xvi., 642.

SIDNEY HOWARD GAY.

SIDNEY HOWARD GAY, for whom some of the class were happy in procuring from the President and Fellows of the University a well-merited degree in 1877, sent the Secretary, in the autumn of 1882, a package of reminiscences, which were placed at his disposal. From these he selects the following.

Hingham is his native place. His father was Ebenezer Gay, and his family have lived in Hingham since the beginning of the last century. The first of the name in Hingham was Dr. Ebenezer Gay (H. C. 1714), who was minister of the parish sixty-nine years and nine months, — the longest ministry on record.

His mother, Mary Allyne Otis, was a daughter of Joseph, a brother of James Otis. "My ancestry, you see," he says, "was the best part of me."

He entered college at fifteen years, but remained only to the beginning of the Junior year, when ill health compelled him to leave. Two years of idleness apparently set him up again, and he was put into the counting-house of Perkins & Co., of Boston. He remained in the employ of that house about two years, almost to the dissolution of the firm. Then, after trying the West for a couple of years, he began the study of law in his father's office at Hingham.

But he soon abandoned the profession, as he says, "from certain scruples of conscience as to the oath to support the Constitution of the United States. For my mind had been turned, by reading history and ethics, to the question of slavery; and I soon reached the conclusion that, if one really believed slavery to be absolutely and morally wrong, he had no right to take an oath to support a constitution that he did not mean to obey because it upheld slavery."

Under the circumstances it was almost inevitable that he should soon drift into that little circle of Abolitionists in Boston, of which Garrison was the head, and Phillips, Quincy, the Jackson brothers Francis and Edmund, Mr. and Mrs. Ellis Gray Loring, the Chapmans, the Westons, the Childs, the Mays, and others, were shining lights. "This handful of people," he says, "to the outside world a set of pestilent fanatics, were among themselves the most charming circle of cultivated men and women that it has ever been my lot to know."

In Anti-Slavery he found the first serious aim of his life. In 1842 he became one of the lecturing agents of the American Anti-Slavery Society, and in 1843 the editor of the Anti-Slavery Standard, the organ of the Society, published in New York. In that position he remained for fourteen years, with Mr. Edmund Quincy, Maria Weston Chapman, and James Russell Lowell as "corresponding editors" in Boston, for most of the time though at different periods.

In 1855 it seemed to Mr. Gay that the "cause" no longer required that he should devote himself exclusively to the Standard. He accordingly joined the staff of the New York Tribune. Early in 1862 he was appointed its managing editor, and so remained until the war was over, — the summer of 1865. He had broken down under the long strain of responsible editorship, and took two years to recover. Henry Wilson said the man deserved well of his country who kept the Tribune a war paper in spite of Greeley.

In 1867 he was asked to take the place of managing editor of the Chicago Tribune. He did so, and remained in that position till the great fire in 1871. In the spring of 1872 he was asked to join the editorial staff of the New York Evening Post. He accepted the invitation, and remained there for two years.

In 1874 a proposal was made to Mr. W. C. Bryant, by Scribner, Armstrong, & Co., to join them in getting out an illustrated History of the United States. He consented, on condition that Mr. Gay would be its author, — as that was a task which Mr. Bryant, at the age of eighty, could not undertake, and which they did not ask. He died before the second volume was published. Two of the three partners also died within the same year, the third was compelled to leave the house, and the publication fell into new hands and a new house. "This," Mr. Gay says, "was not a fortunate concatenation of circumstances."

Excepting a Preface to the first volume, Mr. Bryant did not write, and never intended to write, a single line; while the mistake was made by publishers and subscription agents of attempting to persuade the public that he was the author of a work of one half of which not a word was written until after his death, and the first part of which he never saw until it was in printed pages.

"Whether the work has any merit or not," adds Mr. Gay, "this I may note without immodesty, — that on the appearance of the first volume a new interest has been aroused in American history, which does not seem a mere coincidence; for all the authors who have written, or proposed to write, upon the subject, within the last half-dozen years, have followed the method which I first adopted, and have gone to sources of knowledge which I was the first to use in this country. A new treatment of American history has become popular."

Since the Bryant was finished, two years ago, Mr. Gay's time has been devoted to newspaper literary work, an occasional magazine article, and a volume upon history for young people, just finished. He has begun a volume for Mr. Morse's series of American Statesmen; and another is promised for Warner's series of American Authors.

In 1845, Mr. Gay married Elizabeth, daughter of Daniel Neall, of Philadelphia, and granddaughter of Warner Mifflin, one of the most eminent of the Friends of the last century. They have three living children: Sarah Mifflin, Martin (C. E., graduated, in 1877, at the Massachusetts Institute of Technology), and Mary Otis.

CHARLES WARREN HARTSHORN.

TAUNTON, June 20, 1882.

DEAR HIGGINSON, —
According to my best recollection, I was born at Taunton, October 8, 1814.

After graduation I studied law one year with Hon. Horatio Pratt at Taunton, then one year in the Law School at Cambridge, then one year with Hon. Emory Washburn at Worcester; — was admitted to the bar in 1837, and practised with Mr. Washburn till 1843, then alone for one year; — then with J. C. Bancroft Davis, till October 6, 1847, when I was appointed Clerk of the Supreme Judicial Court for Worcester County, which office I held for five years and declined a reappointment.

I then acted as consulting counsel, referee, and. auditor (not going into court for trial of cases) till July, 1856; when I engaged in the manufacture of letter-envelopes, at Worcester, in which I continued till 1860.

In 1869, I removed to Taunton, where I have remained ever since.

Never married. In the interval between 1860 and 1869 I kept up a partial connection with my former profession, as before, by way of consultation, and acting as referee and auditor, and re-editing my solitary literary bantling, "The New England Sheriff."

Very truly yours,
CHARLES W. HARTSHORN.

WALDO HIGGINSON.

WALDO HIGGINSON, son of Stephen and Louisa (Storrow) Higginson, was born in Boston, May 1, 1814. He was fitted for college chiefly by Mr. William Wells of Cambridge. He also spent a year at the Round Hill School of Messrs. Joseph G. Cogswell and George Bancroft, and was for a time at that of Mr. R. W. Emerson at Cambridge. Graduating in 1833, he spent the subsequent year at the South, chiefly at the home of his brother-in-law, Rev. Dr. Keith of Alexandria, Virginia. In 1834–35 he studied law in the office of Judge Jackson of Boston. In the summer of 1835, he gave up that profession, and entered the office of Col. Loammi Baldwin in Charlestown, as student in Civil Engineering. In the summer of 1837, he accepted the invitation of Mr. W. S. Whitwell, C. E., to go to Georgia on the State Railway across the Alleghanies under charge of Col. S. H. Long, U. S. Topographical Engineers. In the summer of 1839, he left this work to accept the offer of Col. J. M. Fessenden as assistant engineer on the Eastern Railroad between Ipswich and Newburyport. When that work was completed, in 1841, he established himself in Boston as Civil

Engineer and Surveyor, and was there nearly four years. In the spring of 1845 he was chosen Agent and Engineer of the Boston and Lowell Railroad Company, which office he filled till May 18, 1853, when he was suddenly, at the age of thirty-nine, struck down by paralysis. This produced a tedious illness, from which he was long in recovering, and was never fully restored.

In the autumn of 1856, being measurably recovered, he was chosen President of the New England Railroad Mutual Insurance Company. This enterprise was sustained by the best companies in New England, but the President, becoming persuaded in 1859 that the mutual principle of insurance was not adapted to railroads, advised the abandonment of the experiment. This was done, and the company wound up its organization without loss to the insured. In 1860, however, he started a new mutual insurance company designed for manufacturing establishments,—the "Arkwright," of which he was chosen and still remains President. This immediately became successful, and has so continued.

In December, 1845, he married Mary Davies, daughter of William Davies Sohier, of Boston.

At Commencement, 1869, he was chosen Overseer of Harvard University. That office he resigned on Commencement, 1873.

ABIEL ABBOT LIVERMORE.

ABIEL ABBOT LIVERMORE has furnished the following autobiographical sketch.

"I was born in Wilton, N. H., October 30, 1811. My father, Jonathan Livermore, was the eldest son of Rev. Jonathan

Livermore, the first minister of the Congregational Church of that town. My mother, Abigail Abbot, was the daughter of Abiel Abbot, of Wilton. My youth, till I was fifteen, was passed, like that of most country boys, in hard work on the farm in summer, and in the district school in winter. A brother older than myself shared with me these toils and pleasures. Wilton is a picturesque town among bold hills and mountains, and deep valleys, and has a vivid climate, and romantic scenery and surroundings, fitted to tempt forth the imagination and sensibilities of a child.

In 1826 I spent six months in Chelmsford, Mass., with my uncle, after whom I was named, Rev. Abiel Abbot, D. D., and attended the academy kept by Mr. Wallace. In September of the same year, I entered Phillips Academy at Exeter, N. H., then under the care of those eminent teachers, Benjamin Abbot, LL. D., Gideon L. Soule, LL. D., and Joseph Hale Abbot, A. M. Here I passed three years fitting for college, but for two winters I was absent keeping district school in my native town. I was examined and admitted to the freshman class in Harvard College, in 1829, without conditions. While in Cambridge at that time I heard the splendid oration of Orville Dewey before the society of Phi Beta Kappa, and caught some inspiration from his stirring challenge to what is best and highest in man. The first college year was passed in Exeter pursuing the Freshman studies. This was done for the sake of economy. During the four years at Phillips Academy I boarded at the Misses Deborah and Hannah Gilman's, on Water Street. Returning to Cambridge in 1830, and entering the sophomore class unconditioned, the next three years were passed under the gentle and brooding wings of our beloved Alma Mater. Francis Bowen and I roomed together, and boarded the first year, at Mrs. Nichols's, on the northeast corner of the Common, next door east of Dr. Follen's. Our teachers were that wise and sainted band who have long since joined " the choir invisible," — Drs. Hedge, Popkin, Follen, Ware, and Beck; Professors Farrar, Channing, Felton, Peirce, Sales, Bachi, Surault, Barber, Cushing, and Hopkinson; our preachers, Drs. Ware, Palfrey, and Henry Ware, Jr.; and our glorious President, Josiah Quincy.

I graduated in 1833, having as a part at Commencement a Dissertation on "The Effect of Maritime Enterprise on the Character of Nations." During college life I belonged to the Hasty Pudding Club, the Institute of 1770, the religious society, the temperance society, the La Réunion Sociale, and the Phi Beta Kappa.

In 1833 I entered the Cambridge Divinity School, under the instruction of Dr. Ware, Dr. Henry Ware, Jr., and Dr. Palfrey, and had for classmates Samuel P. Andrews, John S. Dwight, George E. Ellis, Oliver C. Everett, Theodore Parker, Reuben Austin, and William Silsbee.

During the last term of the junior year, through the senior year of the undergraduate course, and for three years in the Divinity School, I was engaged in teaching, and fitting boys for college. Among my beloved pupils were George and Thornton K. Ware, Charlotte and Anne Ware, children of Dr. Henry Ware; John F. W. Ware, son of Dr. Henry Ware, Jr.; Frank Rotch, nephew of Mrs. Professor Farrar; Thomas W. Higginson; Charles Devens, late Attorney-General of the United States; Arthur Devens; and Butler of Philadelphia.

Graduating from the Divinity School in 1836, at the age of twenty-five, I received a call to settle in Keene, N. H., and was ordained over the Unitarian Church in that town, November 2, 1836. I was married, May 17, 1838, to Elizabeth D. Abbot, daughter of Rev. Jacob Abbot, of Windham, N. H., who deceased September 13, 1879, after a long and happy married life, though unblessed with living children. While pastor of the Keene Society I published a "Commentary," in three volumes, on the Gospels and Acts of the

Apostles; also a "Review of the Mexican War," and several occasional Discourses; and edited a "Marriage Offering" and Priestley's "Corruptions of Christianity." In April, 1850, I received a call to become the pastor of the Unitarian Society in Cincinnati, Ohio, and removed to that city in May, for the benefit of a milder climate; my health having become impaired by a severe bronchial affection.

In the autumn of 1856 I removed to New York, on an invitation to become the editor of the Christian Inquirer, the organ of the Unitarian faith in that city. I became the pastor of the Unitarian Church in Yonkers on the Hudson. The joint duties of the editorship and the pastorate were fulfilled till the summer of 1863, when I was invited to take the Presidency of the Meadville Theological School, which at the close of the present academical term, in June, 1883, will cover twenty years. Beside the duties of the school, I have completed the "Commentary" on the remaining books of the New Testament, in two volumes, and printed several reviews, sketches of travels, syllabuses of lectures, and occasional sermons.

Thus I empty at your feet this basket of dry straw,— facts, names, dates, places.

One great happiness I have had,— that of mediocrity in talents, position, possessions, influence, name and fame. Ovid was a wise man: "*In medio* tutissimus ibis."

The broad lesson of seventy-one years is gratitude to God and sympathy with man."

MEADVILLE, PENN., November, 1882.

JOSEPH LOVERING.

THE following notice is mainly from "The Harvard Book," published in 1874, with some additions and amendments furnished by Professor Lovering.

Joseph Lovering was born in Charlestown, Massachusetts, on December 25, 1813. He was the son of Robert Lovering, surveyor of ice, wood, and lumber. He attended one of the ordinary grammar schools of his native town until he was fourteen years of age, and went through Colburn's Algebra by himself at this school, his teachers having no knowledge whatever of that subject. On leaving school, he was encouraged by his pastor, Rev. Dr. James Walker (afterwards Professor and President of Harvard College), to fit himself for college, reciting to him daily, and receiving from him in many ways the most valuable aid. He entered the sophomore class of Harvard College in 1830, and graduated with his class in 1833. During his college course he received two appointments for exhibitions, and a mathematical part which was not spoken.

At the Commencement he delivered the Latin Salutatory Oration, which at that time was invariably assigned to the fourth scholar in the scale of rank. This Commencement was made interesting by the fact that it was the last one held in the old church, which stood near the spot now occupied by the Law School. Three years later, when his class were entitled to receive the Master's degree, he delivered the Valedictory Oration in Latin, according to the custom of that day. He was a member of the Davy Club, the Institute, the Hasty Pudding Club, and the $\Phi B K$ Society. During the first year after his graduation, he taught a small private school in Charlestown. In the autumn of 1834 he entered the Divinity School in Cambridge, and remained there for two years. During a part of the academical year 1834-35 he assisted Professor Peirce in the instruction of the College classes in mathematics. In 1835-36 he was Proctor and Instructor in Mathematics, and during a part of the year conducted the morning and evening services in the College Chapel; all those who usually officiated at the devotional exercises of the College being either sick or absent from Cambridge. In 1836-37 he was Tutor in Mathematics, and Lecturer in Natural Philosophy. In 1838 he was made Hollis Professor of Mathematics and Natural Philosophy, a position which he still holds.

In 1853-54 he acted as Regent during Professor Felton's absence in Europe, and in 1857 he succeeded him in that office, and held it until 1870. In consideration of his long and uninterrupted services to the College, he was offered a year's leave of absence in 1868-69, which he passed in Europe.

In 1879, he received from Harvard College, with his classmates Professors Bowen and Torrey, the degree of LL. D.

He was married, in 1844, to Sarah Gray Hawes, of Boston. He has two daughters, Cora Lovering and Eva Lovering. His two sons have graduated at Harvard College; James Walker Lovering in 1866, and Ernest Lovering in 1881.

Although his best time and thoughts were given to his college duties, he found some leisure for other work. At different times he delivered nine courses, of twelve lectures each, on Astronomy or Physics, before the Lowell Institute in Boston; five of which were repeated to a different audience on the days following their first delivery, according to the original practice of that institution. He gave shorter courses of lectures at the Smithsonian Institution in Washington, the Peabody Institute of Baltimore, and the Charitable Mechanics' Institution of Boston, and one or more lectures in many towns and cities of New England.

In 1842 he edited a new edition of Farrar's " Electricity

and Magnetism," at the request of the author. In 1873, he published a thick quarto volume on the Aurora Borealis, in the Memoirs of the American Academy of Arts and Sciences. Other memoirs, on Terrestrial Magnetism, on the Aurora, and on the Determination of Transatlantic Longitudes, have been published by him in the same series.

Besides these more important works, he has contributed a large number of scientific articles and reviews to the Proceedings of the American Academy, to the Proceedings of the American Association for the Advancement of Science, to the American Journal of Science, to the Journal of the Franklin Institute, to the American Almanac, to the North American Review, to the Christian Examiner, to Old and New, and to the Popular Science Monthly.

He was Permanent Secretary of the American Association for the Advancement of Science for nineteen years (between 1854 and 1873), and edited fifteen volumes of its Proceedings. He was also its President in 1873.

He is a member of the American Academy of Arts and Sciences in Boston, was its Corresponding Secretary for many years, afterwards Vice-President, and is now its President. He is also a member of the National Academy of Sciences, of the American Philosophical Society of Philadelphia, and of the Buffalo Historical Society.

From 1867 to 1876 he was connected with the United States Coast Survey, and had charge of the computations for determining differences of longitude in the United States, and across the Atlantic Ocean, by means of the land and cable lines of telegraph.

For some years he has been one of the Trustees of the Tyndall Fund for the endowment of scientific research.

The secretary has been furnished by Professor Lovering with the following catalogue of his publications, together with subjects lectured on, in different years, at the Lowell Institute.

Catalogue of Publications.

1. An Account of the Magnetic Observations made at the Magnetic Observatory of Harvard College. In Two Parts. (Memoirs of the American Academy, Vol. II. pp. 1–160.)
2. On the Secular Periodicity of the Aurora Borealis. (Ibid., Vol. IX. pp. 101–120.)
3. On the Determination of Transatlantic Longitudes by Means of the Telegraphic Cables. (Ibid., Vol. IX. pp. 437–477.)
4. Catalogue of Auroras observed, mostly at Cambridge, after 1838. (Ibid., Vol. X. pp. 1–8.)
5. On the Periodicity of the Aurora Borealis. In Two Parts. (Ibid., Vol. X. pp. 9–351, with plates.)
6. On the Causes of the Difference in the Strength of Ordinary Magnets, and Electro-Magnets, of the same Size and Shape. (Proceedings of the American Academy, Vol. II. p. 105.)
7. On the Law of Continuity. (Ibid., Vol. II. p. 120.)
8. On the Aneroid Barometer. (Ibid., Vol. II. p. 186.)
9. Electrical Experiment. (Ibid., Vol. IV. p. 251.)
10. On the Connection of Electricity with Tornadoes. (Ibid., Vol. II. p. 293.).
11. On Coronæ and Halos. (Ibid., Vol. II. p. 302.)
12. On the Stereoscope. (Ibid., Vol. III. p. 22.)
13. On the Bioscope. (Ibid., Vol. III. p. 106.)
14. Apparatus for Rapid Rotations. (Ibid., Vol. III. p. 107.)
15. Shape of Luminous Spots in Solar Eclipses. (Ibid., Vol. III. p. 160.)
16. Notice of the death of John Farrar. (Ibid., Vol. III. p. 38.)
17. Notice of the death of Melloni. (Ibid., Vol. III. p. 164.)
18. New Apparatus and Experiments in Optics and Acoustics. (Ibid., Vol. III. p. 169.)
19. Arago's Opinion of Table-moving. (Ibid., Vol. III. p. 187.)
20. On Fessel's Gyroscope. (Ibid., Vol. III. p. 206.)
21. Apparatus to regulate the Electric Light. (Ibid., Vol. III. p. 225.)
22. Does the Mississippi River flow up-hill? (Ibid., Vol. III. p. 229.)
23. Report on Hedgcock's Quadrant. (Ibid., Vol. III. p. 384.)
24. On the Boomerang. (Ibid., Vol. IV. p. 12.)
25. Report on Meteorological Observations. (Ibid., Vol. IV. p. 34.)
26. On the Ocean Cable. (Ibid., Vol. IV. p. 79.)

27. On the Polarization of the Light of Comets. (Ibid., Vol. IV. p. 100.)
28. Report on the Polar Expedition of Dr. I. I. Hayes. (Ibid., Vol. IV. pp. 103 and 423.)
29. On Records of the Aurora Borealis. (Ibid., Vol. IV. p. 325.)
30. First Observations of the Aurora in New England. (Ibid., Vol. IV. p. 336.)
31. Notice of the death of Biot. (Ibid., Vol. VI. p. 16.)
32. On the Velocity of Light and the Sun's Distance. (Ibid., Vol. VI. p. 114.)
33. Notice of the death of O. M. Mitchel. (Ibid., Vol. VI. p. 133.)
34. On the Optical Method of studying Sound. (Ibid., Vol. VII. p. 413.)
35. On the Periodicity of the Aurora Borealis. (Ibid. Vol. VIII. p. 55.)
36. On the French Republican Calendar. (Ibid., Vol. VIII. p. 348.)
37. Application of Electricity to the Motion of Tuning Forks. (Ibid., Vol. VIII. p. 53.)
38. On Optical Meteorology. (Ibid., Vol. VIII. p. 213.)
39. On Transatlantic Longitudes. (Ibid., Vol. VIII. p. 502.)
40. Notice of the death of William Mitchell. (Ibid., Vol. VIII. p. 131.)
41. Notice of the death of Faraday. (Ibid., Vol. VIII. p. 31.)
42. Notice of the death of David Brewster. (Ibid., Vol. VIII. p. 38.)
43. Notice of the death of J. F. W. Herschel. (Ibid., Vol. VIII. p. 461.)
44. Notice of the death of Christopher Hansteen. (Ibid., Vol. IX. p. 282.)
45. Notice of the death of Auguste A. de la Rive. (Ibid., Vol. IX. p. 356.)
46. Notice of the death of James Walker. (Ibid., Vol. X. p. 485.)
47. Notice of the death of Joseph Winlock. (Ibid., Vol. XI. p. 339.)
48. Notice of the death of Alexis Caswell. (Ibid., Vol. XII. p. 307.)
49. Notice of the death of John H. Temple. (Ibid., Vol. XIII. p. 449.)
50. Notice of the death of Joseph Henry. (Ibid., Vol. XIV. p. 356.)
51. Notice of the death of H. W. Dove. (Ibid., Vol. XV. p. 383.)
52. Address as President on presenting the Rumford Medal to J. Willard Gibbs. (Ibid., Vol. XVI. p. 292.)
53. Anticipations of the Lissajous Curves. (Ibid., Vol. XVI. p. 415.)

54. Notices of the deaths of Richard H. Dana, of Edward Desor, and of John W. Draper. (Ibid., Vol. XVII. p. 399, &c.)
55. On the Electro-dynamic Forces. (Proceedings of the American Association for the Advancement of Science, Vol. II. p. 278.)
56. On a curious Phenomenon relating to Vision. (Ibid., Vol. II. p. 369.)
57. On a singular Case of Interference in the Eye itself. (Ibid., Vol. VII. p. 23.)
58. On a Modification of Soleil's Polarizing Apparatus. (Ibid., Vol. VII. p. 24.)
59. On the Australian Weapon called the Boomerang. (Ibid., Vol. XII. p. 45.)
60. On the Optical Method of studying Sound. (Ibid., Vol. XVI. p. 25.)
61. On the Periodicity of the Aurora Borealis. (Ibid., Vol. XVI. p. 82.)
62. Sympathetic Vibrations between Tuning-Forks and Stretched Cords. (Ibid., Vol. XVII. p. 103.)
63. On Methods of illustrating Optical Meteorology. (Ibid., Vol. XIX. p. 64.)
64. On Sympathetic Vibrations. (Ibid., Vol. XXI. p. 59, and Journal of Franklin Institute, May, 1873.)
65. Addresses as President at the Portland Meeting. (Ibid., Vol. XXII. pp. 417–427.)
66. On a new Way of illustrating the Vibrations of Air in Organ-Pipes. (Ibid., Vol. XXIII. p. 113.)
67. Address as retiring President. (Ibid., Vol. XXIII. pp. 1–36. Republished in the Popular Science Monthly, American Journal of Science, and the London Philosophical Magazine.)
68. On a new Method of Measuring the Velocity of Electricity. (Ibid., Vol. XXIV. p. 35. Also, Journ. de Physique, Tom. VI. p. 259.)
69. Shooting Stars. (American Journal of Science, Vol. XXXV. p. 323.)
70. The American Prime Meridian. (Ibid., N. S., Vol. IX p. 184.)
71. The Aneroid Barometer. (Ibid., N. S., Vol. IX. p. 249.)
72. On the Velocity of Light and the Sun's Distance. (Ibid., N. S., Vol. XXXVI. p. 161.)
73. Melloni's Researches on Radiant Heat. (American Almanac, 1850, pp. 64–81.)

74. Animal Electricity. (Ibid., 1851, pp. 74–89.)
75. Recent Discoveries in Astronomy. (Ibid., 1852, pp. 66–90.)
76. Comets. (Ibid., 1853, pp. 68–88.)
77. Atmospherical Electricity. (Ibid., 1854, pp. 70–82, and 1855, pp. 65–76.)
78. Lightning and Lightning Rods. (Ibid., 1856, pp. 65–85.)
79. Terrestrial Magnetism. (Ibid., 1857, pp. 67–84.)
80. Theories of Terrestrial Magnetism. (Ibid., 1858, pp. 67–80.)
81. On the Boomerang. (Ibid., 1859, pp. 67–76.)
82. On the Aurora Borealis and Australis. (Ibid., 1860, pp. 55–76.)
83. On Meteorology. (Ibid., 1861, pp. 58–80.)
84. On the Pressure of the Atmosphere and the Barometer. (Ibid., 1862, pp. 42–67.)

REVIEWS.

85. Guyot's Physical Geography. (Christian Examiner, Vol. XLVII. p. 96.)
86. Humboldt's Cosmos. (Ibid., Vol. XLVIII. pp. 53–88.)
87. Skepticism in Science. (Ibid., Vol. LI. pp. 209–250.)
88. Spiritual Mechanics. (Ibid., Vol. LV. pp. 1–21.)
89. Thompson and Kaemtz on Meteorology. (North American Review, Vol. LXXI. pp. 51–99.)
90. Elementary Works on Physical Science. (Ibid., Vol. LXXII. pp. 358–395.)
91. Michael Faraday. (Old and New, Vol. I. p. 47.)
92. Reports on Lighthouses. By Benjamin Peirce and Joseph Lovering. (Journal of the Franklin Institute, Vol. XVIII. p. 249, 1849.)
93. On the Internal Equilibrium and Motion of Bodies. (Cambridge Mathematical Miscellany, Vol. I. pp. 31–41.)
94. On the Application of Mathematical Analysis to Researches in the Physical Sciences. (Ibid., pp. 33–81 and 121–130.)
95. Encke's Comet. (Ibid., pp. 82–92.)
96. The Divisibility of Matter. (Ibid., pp. 169–182.)
97. Boston and Science. (Memorial History of Boston, Vol. IV. pp. 489–526.)
98. Article on the Telegraph. (American Cyclopædia, last edition.)
99. Address at the Dedication of the Mural Monument to the Memory of Dr. James Walker, in the Harvard Church, Charlestown.

SUBJECTS OF LECTURES AT THE LOWELL INSTITUTE.

1840–41. Electricity and Magnetism.
1841–42. Mechanics.
1842–43. Astronomy.
1843–44. Optics.
1845–46. Astronomy.
1853–54. Electricity and Magnetism.
1859–60. Astronomy.
1865–66. Light and Sound.
1879–80. Connection of the Physical Sciences.

He also edited, Memoirs of the American Academy of Arts and Sciences. Six volumes, from V. to X. inclusive, and part of Volume XI.

Also, Proceedings of the same Academy, Volumes VII., VIII, and XVII.

ROBERT TRAILL SPENCE LOWELL.

THE following statement is kindly furnished by Robert T. S. Lowell, under date of Schenectady, July 5, 1882.

"After graduation, I went through a full course of medicine without taking a degree. In 1835 or 1836 went into business under my eldest brother. After leaving that occupation, went to Schenectady to study for holy orders, under Rev. Dr. A. Potter, then lately from St. Paul's Church, Boston. Meeting the Bishop of Newfoundland (with Bermuda), Dr. Spencer, went, at his suggestion, to be ordained by him in Bermuda, having already passed examination and being about to be ordained by Bishop Griswold of Massachusetts. Was ordained Deacon in 1842 and Priest in 1843, and appointed domestic chaplain to the Bishop. Asked for and got an appointment to Bay Roberts, Newfoundland, as missionary under the English Society for Propagating the Gospel. Came home and married Mary Ann, eldest daughter of James Duane, of Duane. After a famine in which I broke down by serving and sharing with my parishioners, having received the thanks of the Colonial Secretary, came home. By appointment of Bishop Doane, began a mission in a poor quarter of Newark, N. J., rebuilt a beautiful little church, and after eleven years' service, chiefly among the poor, in 1859 accepted the rectorship of Christ Church, Duanesburg, N. Y., a parish founded by Judge Duane, my wife's great-grandfather, who was appointed by Washington United States District Judge in New York, by the same act by which my own grandfather, John Lowell, was appointed to the same office in Massachusetts. In 1868, chosen Professor of Belles-Lettres in Racine College, Wisconsin, but declined. After ten years' work among the farmers at Duanesburg, accepted the headmastership of St. Mark's School, Southborough, Mass. In 1873 was chosen Professor of Latin Language and Literature in Union University, Schenectady, N. Y., and in 1879 resigned that place.

"Have published the following: —

The New Priest in Conception Bay (several moderate editions).
Fresh Hearts that failed Three Thousand Years ago, and other Poems.
Poems by Author of "The New Priest," &c.
Antony Drade, a Story of a School.
A Story or Two from an Old Dutch Town.

"Of course many stray things in prose and verse, of which, perhaps, I may mention the Harvard Commemoration Hymn, which Mr. Thomas Hughes has quoted several times, a hymn for the dedication of the Town Hall in Southborough, Mass., and a poem for the Centennial Celebration by the citizens of Saratoga County of the battle (with Burgoyne) at Bemis Heights."

Mr. Lowell also writes, October 20, 1882, that he has six children living, as follows: —

Perceval (H. C. 1870), now General Passenger Agent of the Chicago, Burlington, and Quincy Railroad.

James Duane (H. C. 1874, and Lawrence S. S. 1877), now among the miners in Colorado.

Charles is Manager of the Bombay Branch of the Comptoir d'Escompte de Paris.

Robert Traill Spence (Union C. 1880) is in Chicago in the service of the Chicago, Burlington, and Quincy Railroad.

And two daughters, Mary Anna and Rebecca Russell.

None of his children are married.

WILLIAM MACK.

THE secretary has received the following notice of this classmate, from a well-informed and judicious chronicler.

"William Mack, son of Elisha and Catherine Sewall Pynchon (Orne) Mack, was born in Salem, Mass., August 11, 1814. Prepared for college at the Latin Grammar School, Salem, then under the charge of Theodore Eames, Esq. Graduated at Harvard University in the class of 1833. The two years following his graduation, was a teacher in New Bedford, Mass. In 1835 commenced the study of medicine with John C. Warren, M. D., of Boston; the last year of his medical course, the House Surgeon in Massachusetts General Hospital; received the degree of M. D. in 1838, at Harvard.

"Passed two years in Europe, devoting his time to his professional studies in Paris, to visiting the hospitals and schools in some of the principal cities, and to foreign travel.

"He returned to this country in the autumn of 1840, and

commenced the practice of the profession in Salem, where he has continued to the present time, taking a leading position among the physicians and surgeons of this city and its vicinity.

"He has always been interested in the scientific and literary institutions of his native place, and in some of them held prominent positions; and has also rendered assistance to the promotion of some of the industries that have from time to time been introduced."

GEORGE HENRY NICHOLS.

BOSTON, August 23, 1882.

DEAR WALDO, — I will with pleasure answer your questions.

I was born in Portland, Me., August 26, 1814. I entered Exeter Academy, August, 1825. I entered Harvard College, August, 1829. After leaving college, having adopted the medical profession, I graduated at the University of Pennsylvania, March, 1836, after two years' study there, having previously studied one year at Bowdoin College. Was married, November, 1836, to Sarah A. Atherton, of Portland, Me. Practised my profession in Buffalo, N. Y., about one year and a half. Removed to Standish, Me., June, 1839. Practised there twenty years. Removed to Boston, June, 1859, where I still reside, in the same street to which I at first came. Have had six children; three are living at this date.

Sincerely your friend,

GEO. H. NICHOLS.

The secretary adds to the above the following: —

The eldest son of Dr. Nichols is Dr. John T. G. Nichols, well known as a physician in Cambridge. He took a medical degree at Harvard in 1859, and has long been upon the Examining Board of the University appointed by the Overseers. He married a daughter of Dr. Gilman, of Portland, Me., and has now three children. A younger son, W. A. Nichols, graduated at the Lawrence Scientific School in 1865, and is holding an important post in the Engineering Department of New York City. He is unmarried.

The only surviving daughter married F. L. Hills, a West Point graduate, who has now a responsible position on the New York and New England Railroad. They have three children. A younger daughter married R. C. Johnson (H. C. 1864), and died some years ago, leaving two children.

So that our classmate has eight grandchildren.

WILLIAM DANDRIDGE PECK.

WILLIAM DANDRIDGE PECK, after graduating, studied medicine with Dr. George Cheyne Shattuck (the first of that name), of Boston, completing his preparatory studies with Dr. Wilder, of Leominster, Mass. On taking his degree as M. D., he accepted an invitation of Dr. Kendall, an old physician of Sterling, Mass., to begin practice there as his partner. In 1838 he married Elizabeth, daughter of Dr. Wilder. She died in 1853, leaving two daughters. Two years after her death, he married Mary Esther Willard, of Sterling, by whom he had another daughter, born in 1871. He gave up practice a few years after his first marriage, and thenceforth devoted himself to the affairs of the town and county. In connection with that useful avocation, he has been a director in various important institutions whose central offices were in the cities of Worcester and Fitchburg. In 1848 and 1849, and again in 1854, he represented Sterling in the General Court, and in 1859 he was in the State Senate.

WILLIAM MACKAY PRICHARD.

WILLIAM MACKAY PRICHARD, after graduating, chose the profession of the law. He studied in New York City with Mr. William Emerson (H. C. 1818). On being admitted to the bar, he formed a partnership with that gentleman. This continued until Judge Emerson gave up practice and retired to spend his last years with his younger brother, Ralph Waldo, at Concord, Mass. Mr. Prichard next formed a connection with William G. Choate (H. C. 1852). This lasted until Mr. Choate was appointed United States District Judge.

The law firm as originally formed, of Emerson and Prichard, and continued to the present time with younger men, of which Mr. Prichard has long been senior partner, has always maintained an eminently respectable and thoroughly reliable position at the New York Bar.

Mr. Prichard married, in April, 1852, Miss Eliza Plummer, of New York City.

EDWARD JOSIAH STEARNS.

FAULKLAND, DEL., September 7, 1882.

MY DEAR HIGGINSON, —
I send you herewith, as I promised you two or three months ago, "the most important facts of my life."

Born in Bedford, Middlesex County, Mass., Feb. 24, 1810; brought up a Puritan of "the straitest sect"; prepared for College, first at the Academy at Concord, where I boarded in the family of John Thoreau, father of Henry David (or, as he was then called, David Henry) Thoreau, — afterwards at the

Warren Academy, Woburn; entered the freshman class at Amherst at the beginning of the third term, May, 1830; entered sophomore at Harvard in September of the same year; after graduating, went to Norfolk, Va.; taught in a private family there, from September to February, and (as you may remember) in a classical school in Alexandria, D. C., from March to August; had charge, the next year, of a classical school at the "Five Corners," Dorchester, Mass.; entered the Theological Seminary at Andover, October, 1835; left there the following January, and studied in private; "licensed to preach" by the Woburn Association, April, 1836; in 1839, "Preceptor" of the Fuller Academy, West Newton; became a Churchman that year; ordained Deacon by Bishop Griswold, on Trinity Sunday, 1840, in St. Mary's Church, Newton Lower Falls, and took charge of St. James's Church, Amesbury; 1841, Professor in Jubilee College, Peoria County, Illinois; 1842, instructor in a young ladies' school, Richmond, Va.; 1843, ordained Priest by Bishop Whittingham, the fourth Sunday in Advent, in St. Peter's Church, Baltimore, and became Rector of Grace Church, Elk Ridge Landing, Md.; 1845, Professor in the College of St. James, near Hagerstown; 1846, Professor in the Baltimore "Central Male High School" (now City College); 1847, Rector of St. Peter's Church, Ellicott City; 1849, Professor in St. John's College, Annapolis; 1853, instructor in a classical school in Philadelphia; 1854, Professor in St. Timothy's Hall, Catonsville, near Baltimore; 1856, Submaster of the Public Latin School, Boston; 1857, in ill health and laid on the shelf; 1858, instructor in Mystic Hall Seminary for Young Ladies, West Medford; 1859, again at St. Timothy's, Catonsville; July, 1860, to May, 1861, at my mother's in Bedford, she being paralytic and bed-ridden, and my brother, Elijah W. (class of 1838), having had a leg amputated, and lying hovering between life and death, all that autumn and winter; April 22, hanged and burned in effigy in my native place by certain "lewd fellows of the baser sort," and some more respectable ones gone crazy by the war; it did them good, and did n't hurt me; May 1, went from Bedford to Newark, N. J., and took charge of The House of Prayer, in the absence of the Rector in Europe (in the Vestry were United States Senator Wright and Ex-Governor Price); September 26 (being the Fast Day appointed by President Lincoln) preached a sermon entitled "The Sword of the Lord," from Jer. xlvii. 6; September 30, left Newark for Baltimore; at the request of friends there and in Newark, published the sermon, through Waters, Baltimore; it went rapidly to the third edition, more than twelve hundred copies being sold in a few weeks; 1862, Rector of St. Paul's Parish, Centreville, Md.; February 2, fourth Sunday after Epiphany, preached a sermon entitled "The Powers that Be," from the epistle for the day, Rom. xiii. 1; this was also published by Waters; 1864, again at St. Timothy's, Catonsville; 1866, instructor in a classical school at Cambridge, Md.; 1868, Chaplain of the Maryland Hospital for the Insane; 1869, Associate Editor of Bledsoe's Southern Review; 1870, in charge of Trinity Parish, Elkton, Md., in the absence of the Rector; 1871 to 1878, Rector of St. Mary's Whitechapel Parish, Denton, Md.

Since 1878 I have been pretty much laid on the shelf, except with my pen. Among its productions, besides those already mentioned, are these: —

Notes on Uncle Tom's Cabin. Philadelphia: Lippincott, 1853. 12mo, pp. 210.

Afterpiece to the Comedy of Convocation. Hartford: Church Press Company, 1870. 16mo, pp. 168.

Birth and New Birth: A New Treatment of an Old Subject. Second Edition. Baltimore: George Lycett, 1873. 16mo, pp. 122.

The Faith of Our Forefathers, being an Examination of Archbishop Gibbons's "Faith of Our Fathers." New York: T. Whittaker, 1879. Fifth Edition, 1881. 12mo, pp. 380.

The Archbishop's Champion brought to Book. New York: T. Whittaker, 1881. 16mo, pp. 122.

You will see from the foregoing that I have been a rolling stone, gathering no moss. Cause, — inability to

> "Lick absurd pomp,
> And crook the pregnant hinges of the knee,
> Where thrift may follow fawning."

You will see, further, from the date of this, that I have changed my residence. Faulkland is seven miles and a half from Wilmington by the Delaware Western Railroad. If you ever come to Wilmington, don't fail to come out here and pay me a visit. You will find a hearty welcome.

If I am alive and well, I shall endeavor to be with you next Commencement. But there's a good deal in that "if," for I have not the strength that I had a year ago. That I have lasted as long as I have, is in the teeth of the doctrine of the "survival of the fittest"; but I don't believe in that doctrine, at least where mind and heart enter into the problem.

I remain, your old classmate and friend,

EDWARD J. STEARNS.

HENRY WARREN TORREY.

CAMBRIDGE, May 21, 1883.

MY DEAR HIGGINSON, —
In compliance with your request, I send you a few biographical notes. My life has not been eventful enough for a long record.

Having spent, after taking my degree, four years in teaching, and in work on Leverett's Latin Lexicon, I removed to New Bedford, and began to study law. After being admitted to the bar in 1840, I returned to my previous occupation of teaching. This calling I have followed in school or in college, with little interruption, to the present time.

From 1844 to 1848 I was a tutor in Harvard College; from 1848 to 1856 I kept a private school for girls in Boston; and from 1856 I have been McLean Professor of History in Harvard College.

Very truly yours,
H. W. TORREY.

In 1879, Professor Torrey received from the College, with his classmates Professors Bowen and Lovering, the degree of LL. D.

NATHANIEL SAVILLE TUCKER.

PEORIA, ILL., July 1, 1882.

DEAR HIGGINSON,—
After getting my degree of M. D. in 1837, I practised medicine in South Boston for a short time.

In 1840 I came to Peoria, where I acted as county physician for about two years; then went into the drug business.

In 1866 my partner and myself gave up the drug business, and since then we have been loaning money, looking after our real estate, and other matters.

Our firm of Tucker and Mansfield is the oldest in the city, we having been connected in business over forty years.

I was never married, which sometimes I regret and sometimes I do not.

Regretting that the details are so meagre and commonplace, I remain, with regards to the class,

Yours very truly,
N. S. TUCKER.

WINSLOW MARSTON WATSON.

WINSLOW MARSTON WATSON, soon after graduating, chose the calling of a journalist. After fledging his wings in Boston he went to Troy, N. Y., and his subsequent career is described in the following communications.

WASHINGTON, D. C., June 29, 1882.

MY DEAR HIGGINSON, —

Your favor of the 27th is at hand. In reply, "I have the honor to state," as we used to say, or write, in the Treasury Department, that I was editor of the "Troy Daily Whig" from December, 1839, to July, 1845; of the "Albany Statesman," and "Albany Express," from 1846 to 1850; of the "Syracuse Star" from 1850 to 1852, when I came to Washington; from which city I corresponded with the "New York Express" from 1852 to 1869. The American Organ was published in 1855 and 1856. I was connected with it more in a financial than an editorial capacity.

In 1860 I was one of the editors of the "Union Guard," a campaign paper in the interest of Bell and Everett. During the past ten years I have written many articles for the "Washington Sunday Herald." I was a very warm politician for many years, but now I feel very much like poor Dr. Maginn when he wrote for the "Noctes" these lines: —

> "He would bore us with gabber critical
> About your curst scribes of verse or prose.
> Send him to rest with the unpolitical,
> I never would wish to get drunk with those."

From April, 1861 to August, 1869 I was in the War and Treasury Departments, and for two or three years thereafter in the Congressional Library and Census Office.

P. S. Early this morning I was dreaming of our Alma Mater. I am glad to hear the "old lady" is more flourishing than ever. Give my love to her.

I am your sincere friend,
WINSLOW M. WATSON.

Under date of Washington, July 21, he writes: —

"My wife and I were married in Grace Church, Newark, N. J., by Rev. John Lee Watson, August 9, 1852. Her name was Louisa E. Gibbons, a daughter of James Gibbons, who came from Oxfordshire, England, to Albany, N. Y., in 1792. His wife, Esther Robinson, a native of Windsor, was often patted on the head by old Queen Charlotte, when a child, as she walked along the Castle terrace. . . . . I copy from 'Annals of Albany' the following notice of Mr. Gibbons: 'February 8, 1826, James Gibbons, Alderman of the Fifth Ward, died. If ever a worthy man died, he was that man. In the language of Burns, 'he had the patent of his honors immediately from Almighty God.' In every sense of the word his loss will be severely felt.'"

CHARLES ALFRED WELCH.

BOSTON, November 8, 1882.

DEAR HIGGINSON, —
I taught Latin and Greek at the "Academical Department of the University of Maryland," in Baltimore, one year, commencing a week or so after I graduated. It went by the name of Baltimore College in common parlance. I commenced the study of the law in Baltimore, while I was a teacher, in the year 1834; then studied two terms at the

Law School of Harvard University; went to Springfield in the summer, not being well, and studied that summer, say about four months, with Bliss and Dwight. Mr. Bliss was afterwards President of the Western Railroad. Mr. William Dwight, as you knew, subsequently engaged in manufacturing, and was treasurer of certain mills. I ended off in Sprague and Gray's office, and was admitted to the bar at the April term of the Court of Common Pleas in Suffolk County, Mass. This term ended May 17, 1837, but the record does not show the date of my admission. I went into partnership with Edward D. Sohier, in March, 1838, and the partnership has continued unchanged, without addition or subtraction, from that date to this, over forty-four years, and I suppose will so continue till death closes the concern.

Perhaps I should add, that I was born January 30, 1815; went to Latin School in September, 1823, a few months before I was nine years old, and was always frightened when asked my age till I became nine, the legal age for entering; remained at Latin School six years, the last year being what was then called a resident graduate.

August 20, 1844, I married Mary Love Boott, daughter of Kirk Boott, of Lowell; have two children, Charles A. Welch, who seems lately to have retired from business, and Francis C. Welch, a member of the bar of Suffolk County, who before studying law was for some years at Washington College, of which that distinguished man, Robert E. Lee, was President.

I believe that this answers all your questions.

Yours truly,
CHARLES A. WELCH.

THOMAS WIGGLESWORTH.

THOMAS WIGGLESWORTH, born and bred in Boston, has always lived in that city.

After graduating, in 1833, he read law for about two years, at Northampton, and in the office of Hon. Charles G. Loring of Boston. But preferring commerce to law, he went into his father's counting-room on India Wharf, and became a merchant.

He continued in business for many years, but gradually gave it up, and occupied himself with the care of property, his own and others', and the various trusts incident thereto.

He is a cultivated and liberal patron of art. He has also responded readily to the demands of his Alma Mater.

He has never married.

W. H.

MORRILL WYMAN.

I WAS born, July 25, 1812, in Chelmsford, Middlesex County, Mass. I am the second son of Rufus Wyman and Ann (Morrill) Wyman. My father was born in Woburn, Mass., in 1778, and died in Roxbury, Mass., in 1842. My mother, a daughter of Deacon James Morrill, was born in Boston in 1784, and died in Roxbury in 1843.

In 1818 my father moved to the McLean Asylum in Charlestown as its first physician and superintendent, and here was my home for seventeen years. My early education was first with my brothers at the town school in Charlestown, then in Lexington under the care of Rev. Caleb Stetson, then in a private school in Charlestown. After a year at an academy in Chelmsford, I went in 1827, with my brother Jeffries, to Phillips Exeter Academy, entered Harvard College in 1829, under President Quincy, and was graduated in regular course in 1833.

The next Monday morning after graduation I reported for duty as an Assistant Engineer on the Boston and Worcester Railroad to its Chief Engineer, Col. John M. Fessenden. I was then not in good health, but my active duties as an assistant on a railroad on which no rail had as yet been laid, and the open air life, were of great use to me. After a little more than a year's work, finding my health improved, and having earned sufficient money with economy to make it safe for me to attempt the study of a profession, in the autumn of 1834 I entered my name as a medical student with Dr. William Johnson Walker, an eminent physician and surgeon of Charlestown. Under Dr. Walker I studied in the usual manner of those days, reading such books as men presented to me, and seeing such cases as came to my instructor's office, and occasionally visiting with him a few of his other patients, while making his usual medical visits. Listening to the observations and teachings of a most acute observer, and being directed to the best sources of information as to the particular case, I enjoyed opportunities now seldom offered to medical students. At the same time I attended the winter courses of Lectures in the Medical School of Harvard University. In 1836 I was appointed House Physician to the Massachusetts General Hospital, residing within its walls one year, and was admitted to the degree of Doctor in Medicine at the Commencement following. On the 14th of September of the same year (1837), I went to Cambridge to establish myself in the practice of medicine and surgery, and there I have remained to the present time.

On the 14th of August, 1839, I was married to Elizabeth Aspinwall Pulsifer, daughter of Captain Robert Starkey

Pulsifer, a Boston shipmaster; with her presence I am still blessed. I was elected a member of the American Academy of Arts and Sciences, June 9, 1843, and in 1856 Adjunct Hersey Professor of the Theory and Practice of Medicine in Harvard College Medical School. From 1875 to the present time I have been an Overseer of the College, having been elected for two successive full terms.

In 1850 I invented and gave to my profession a method of removing fluids from the various cavities of the body, especially the chest. It consists essentially of a "trocar and cannula" of a very small diameter fitted to an "exhausting syringe." By these means an operation before considered as always dangerous, and often fatal, has been rendered effectual, safe, and almost painless. In various forms it has gone into general use, and has been applied to a much larger variety of cases than was at first suggested. I hope it may give relief and restore to health the subjects of disease long after my name shall have been forgotten.

My children are: Elizabeth Aspinwall, born July 23, 1840, died March 2, 1862; Anna Morrill,[1] born July 23, 1840; Morrill, born July 10, 1855; Jeffries, born June 15, 1859, died August 26, 1860.

MORRILL WYMAN.

CAMBRIDGE, February 15, 1883.

---

[1] Married Charles F. Walcott, Esq., of the Boston Bar, and has children.

NOTE TO PAGE 99. — William Page Andrews devotes much time to letters, and is a poet. The poems of Jones Very, published many years ago under the auspices of Mr. R. W. Emerson, have just been republished, with an introductory memoir by Mr. Andrews, written in good taste and eloquently.

LIST OF STUDENTS,

SOME TIME IN THE CLASS OF 1833, WHO DID NOT GRADUATE WITH IT.

*Amory, George William.
Baillio, Gervais.
*Baldwin, Loammi.
*Carter, James.
*Dunkin, Christopher.
* ones, William Augustus.
*Joy, John Benjamin.
*Keating, Horace.
King, Rufus Tilden.
*Lawrence, Rufus Bigelow.
*Moody, William Henry.
*Murdock, John.
*Oliver, Francis Eben.
*Parker, Lucius.
*Pray, Isaac Clark.
*Prescott, Thomas Oliver.
*Shimmin, William.
*Temple, Henry Waring Latane.

NOTICES OF STUDENTS,

SOME TIME IN THE CLASS OF 1833, WHO DID NOT GRADUATE WITH IT.

GEORGE WILLIAM AMORY.

GEORGE WILLIAM AMORY was born on the 23d of November, 1814. He entered college from Milton, Mass. His name appears on the annual catalogue only in the freshman and sophomore years. During the former he was the chum of Charles A. Welch.

Soon after leaving college, he went to Evansville, Ind., where his family had extensive landed property. Here he married Mary Phillips, of Utica, N. Y. He remained at Evansville about twenty years. He then returned to Massachusetts, and soon established himself at the Coolidge House, Bowdoin Square, Boston, where he spent the rest of his life, and where he died on the 7th of October, 1882.

When after the war the Harvard Alumni proposed to build Memorial Hall at Cambridge, he generously subscribed and paid $1,000 towards the sum raised for that purpose, the largest gift from any individual credited to the class.

He had three sons. Of these the eldest, John Lowell Amory, lived in Evansville, where he married. He died there in 1872, leaving five children. The other two, Francis and George Kirkland Amory, now live with their mother at the Coolidge House. The youngest of these, George K., is a member of the Nebraska Bar.

GERVAIS BAILLIO.

AS nothing has been heard directly from this classmate, the secretary here inserts the substance of a letter written in 1858 by Mr. Baillio, which gives the record of his life to that date.

He went home to Louisiana in the early part of the senior year, and became engaged in marriage, while fully intending to return and graduate with the class. His mother was so much opposed to his going back, however, that he abandoned his intention, purchased a tract of wild land, married, and became a planter.

For twelve years, from 1839 to 1851, he resided in the parish of Avoyelles, and for seven years, from 1839 to 1846, was Parish Judge. This office, now abolished, involved a multiplicity of arduous duties, both judicial and ministerial, the chief of which were those of probate. In 1851, finding his plantation, near Alexandria, required more of his personal attention, he returned to it. He wrote from this plantation, situated in his native parish of Rapides, which in point of resources and wealth ranks as the third in the State, and contains a population second to none in intelligence and refinement.

He has had ten children, six sons and four daughters; the eldest a son then of about twenty-five years of age, the youngest a son born the 7th of April, 1858. His eldest son lived with him, and assisted in his planting affairs. His second had a taste for mechanics, and was, when the letter was written, on his way to a machine-shop at Mount Vernon, Ohio. His third was at one of the Missouri colleges; and the rest of his children were under his own roof.

In July, 1882, wishing to hear from this wise old classmate, the secretary wrote to the Postmaster at Alexandria, La., to inquire about him, and received the following answer: —

ALEXANDRIA, LA., July 28, 1882.

MY DEAR SIR, — Your communication to the Postmaster at this place, making inquiry of my father, Gervais Baillio, has been duly received, and in reply I am happy to say that he still lives, enjoys robust health, is in the seventy-second year of his age, splendidly preserved, and weighs about two hundred and twenty-five pounds.

My dear old father remembers you well as a dear friend and classmate, and desires me to say that he recalls with pleasure the sweet reminiscences of the "Coffee Club."[1]

He is off in haste from home in the morning, and requests that I inform you that as soon as he returns it will afford him great pleasure to respond to your much appreciated inquiry.

I am his youngest child, (am twenty-four years of age,) and it is I to whom he has intrusted the acknowledgment of your remembrance. Hoping to be honored with a letter from you, at your earliest convenience,

I am, yours very respectfully,
WM. L. BAILLIO.

MR. WALDO HIGGINSON, Boston, Mass.

I answered this cordial letter — addressing the father — on August 20, 1882, giving a full account of all the changes in his circle of friends that I supposed would interest him.

Receiving no answer, I wrote again, and have done so repeatedly, but still no reply.

Whatever may have been the reasons which led to this silence, it is certain that to those who knew Mr. Baillio at Cambridge he must always remain a fitting type of Terence's

"Antiqua homo virtute ac fide."

---

[1] The "Coffee Club" consisted of Baillio, Higginson, Jackson, and Stone, and met every week.

LOAMMI BALDWIN.

LOAMMI BALDWIN was the son of B. F. Baldwin, and nephew of those distinguished civil engineers, Loammi, James F., and George R. Baldwin. His grandfather, Colonel Loammi Baldwin, commanded a regiment in the Revolution, and early in this century was intrusted by the proprietors with superintending the construction of the Middlesex Canal.

Our classmate's name appears on the annual catalogue only in the freshman and sophomore years. After leaving college, he followed for a few years the family calling in this vicinity. He then went West, and bought land in Scott County, Illinois. Here he became a farmer, continuing to pursue engineering as opportunity offered. He suddenly died, of disease of the heart, on the 1st of March, 1855. In 1847 he had married Helen Avery, of the same county in Illinois, who survived him, but died in 1858. They had two children, a son and a daughter. The son, Loammi F., adopted the profession of the family, and is at present a mining engineer in California. The daughter, Mary E., married Mr. Darius Mathewson, of Pomfret, Conn., where she now resides.

JAMES CARTER.

JAMES CARTER entered College at Commencement, 1829, from Lancaster, Mass., and died, much lamented, at Cambridge, March 20, 1830.

CHRISTOPHER DUNKIN.

THE following obituary of this distinguished classmate appeared in the Boston Daily Advertiser of January 29, 1881. It was written by Professor Bowen, who was, during Mr. Dunkin's residence in Cambridge, his intimate companion.

Those who have still some remembrance of the interior history of Harvard College, and of society in Cambridge, from 1832 to 1836, must have read with sorrow the recent announcement of the death of the Hon. Christopher Dunkin, a judge of one of the higher courts in Canada, aged sixty-eight years. He died at Knowlton, near Montreal, January 6, 1881, and his remains were brought to McGill College, of which he had long been one of the governing body and in whose affairs he had taken much interest. Most of the members of the bench and the bar, as well as the faculty of the college, attended his public funeral there on the 11th, either as pall-bearers or mourning spectators, the coffin being borne to Christ Church Cathedral, where the last rites were performed and interment took place. A meeting of the bar was also held and resolutions were passed, expressing the respect and affection with which they had long regarded the deceased.

Those who were his friends in his early youth will be struck with the contrast between this dignified termination of his career, ripe in years and honors, and its brilliant but checkered beginning here at Harvard, almost exactly half a century ago. They first knew him as a precocious and vivacious English boy, fluent in speech and attractive in manners, who had already won for himself, in two universities in the mother country, a high reputation for scholarship and talent, and who evidently cherished a firm purpose of becoming still more distinguished in his new home. Born in London, the only son of a widow with small means, he entered the University of Glasgow at the age of fifteen, and carried off its highest honors at the end of a twelvemonth, as the first prizeman of his year. Seeking a new field for effort, he spent the next year at the University of London, then just created, with high expectations by the liberal party, as an offset to the aristocratic and Tory institutions at Oxford and Cambridge. Here also he succeeded, being declared first scholar of his class during the single year that he remained with them. During this period his frequent amusement was to attend the strangers' gallery in the House of Commons, in order to hear the debates; and being conscious of his own marvellous command of language in extemporaneous talk, he here first formed and nursed his great ambition of becoming a distinguished debater and statesman. One may smile at so lofty a purpose to be cherished by a mere boy; but it betokened a generous disposition. Meanwhile his mother had married again, and his stepfather, Dr. Jonathan Barber, having emigrated to this country, was appointed teacher of elocution here at Harvard in 1829, an office for which, in spite of some eccentricities of manner, he had peculiar and high qualifications. I could point out some distinguished clergymen and lawyers in our neighborhood who were indebted for their first success in the pulpit and at the bar to the enthusiasm for the art of rhetorical delivery which was created here by the lectures of Dr. Barber. Naturally young Dunkin followed his mother by emigrating to this country and coming to her home at Cambridge, where he was matriculated in his third university by becoming a member in its junior year of the class which had entered as freshmen in 1829. Respected by all his Harvard classmates for his brilliant talents and amiable character, he was a great favorite with a few of them, who soon became his particular friends because they sympathized with his tastes, appreciated his literary attainments, and liked his enthusiasm. He was sanguine, ambitious, and perhaps a little vain; with such antecedents, he would have been more than mortal if some boyish vanity had not been developed in him. Frank and cheery in temperament, cordial in his manners, generous in disposition, a lively talker and a delightful companion, he was a being made to be admired and loved by all who really came to know him.

But his great gift, as I have already intimated, was his wonderful fluency and correctness of speech on the spur of the moment. Give him any topic whatever for disquisition or debate, and he would discourse upon it for the hour together, often in stately and ornate diction, and always with so correct use of language, that, if his words had been taken down by a stenographer, and printed just as he uttered them, the verbal critic would have had no fault to find with them. Edward Everett himself, no mean proficient in this difficult art, after once hearing Dunkin lecture extemporaneously, as he always did, remarked: "He must be bewitched to be able to talk thus, for he certainly bewitches his audience." What debates we had in the Harvard Union, a college debating society in those days, when Dunkin was our premier, our William Pitt, our "leader of the house."

He did not graduate, the routine of fixed hours and set tasks being burdensome to him, and the pleasure and profit of lecturing at country lyceums, then in their first gloss of novelty and popularity, induced him to leave college early in his senior year. Thus he spent about a year in each of three different universities, and graduated in neither. But Harvard almost immediately gave him an honorary degree, and appointed him Tutor in Greek before he was twenty-one years old. He was abundantly qualified for the post in point of scholarship, but in every other respect the appointment was a mistake, both for him and for the College. As a foreigner, far more conversant with the customs and manners of British than of American universities, he did not understand the nature of Yankee undergraduates in those days, who were the most kindly fellows in the world with an instructor whom they liked, but a perfect nest of hornets to one who was unpopular on account of his youth and his nationality, and who was also sensitive in temperament. A series of petty annoyances followed, which were perhaps too sternly repressed by the Faculty, and so the rebellion of 1834 broke out, the most formidable tempest in a teapot which Cambridge has witnessed during the present century. Dunkin was made unhappy by it, but he manfully withstood the storm, and continued to be tutor for a second year after the excitement had passed away. Meanwhile a family attachment had sprung up, and in 1835 he married the daughter of his stepfather, the lady who was the joy and light of his home for his whole subsequent life, and who survives him to mourn her great bereavement.

Leaving Cambridge soon after his marriage, he began the study of law, and we next hear of him as private secretary of the Hon. Charles Buller, the associate of Earl Durham in the government of Canada after the Papineau rebellion in that Province in 1837. He aided Buller in drawing up the famous "Canada Report," which prepared the way for the establishment of virtual autonomy in the government of the English colonies. The recall of Earl Durham put an end to this engagement, and Mr. Dunkin then applied himself earnestly and successfully to his practice at the bar. His great ability as an advocate in the courts soon became manifest, and he justly acquired an eminent place in the profession, and was henceforward a prosperous man. After a while his ambition for a political career was kindled afresh. He was elected to the Canadian Parliament, became a member of the ministry, and took a leading share in the debates on the perplexing questions respecting the clergy reserves and the conversion of the feudal tenures. But experience proved that his organization was too delicate and his tastes too refined for the coarse details and intrigues of colonial politics, and he gladly withdrew to the comparative quiet of his labors at the bar. Promotion to the bench soon followed, and the remainder of his career was honored, prosperous, and uneventful. He had gathered around him many associates and loving friends in the home of his maturer years; but by none of these will his death be more regretted, or his memory be more fondly cherished, than by those who were his companions and admirers during his youthful career at Harvard just half a century ago.

ONE OF HIS CLASSMATES.

Cambridge, January 27, 1881.

WILLIAM AUGUSTUS JONES.

WILLIAM AUGUSTUS JONES was with the class only part of the freshman year. After leaving Cambridge, he went into a counting-room, and became a commission merchant in Cincinnati and New Orleans, afterwards a planter in Texas, where he died. He married and had children.

JOHN BENJAMIN JOY.

JOHN BENJAMIN JOY was the son of Benjamin and Hannah (Barrell) Joy, and was born in Boston, January 3, 1814. Joseph Barrell, the father of Mrs. Joy, owned and occupied the farm at Somerville, Mass., afterwards the property of the McLean Asylum for the Insane. His house was the large central building of the group now used by that institution.

Mr. Benjamin Joy died, September 14, 1829, just at the commencement of his son's college life. Our classmate's name appears only on the roll of the freshman year, and again in the senior year, as a university student. In the latter year he had the apartments on Harvard Street subsequently taken and still occupied by the Porcellian Club. Of this society he was a prominent member.

After leaving Cambridge, he returned to Boston. He never studied any profession or engaged in any business.

On the 6th of January, 1835, he married Ellen Marion, daughter of Hon. Stephen White, of Salem, Mass. They had six children, but one only survived them, Charles H. Joy, now the head of the house of Joy, Lincoln, and Motley, selling agents for several large manufacturing establishments.

Mr. Joy was an intimate friend of Fletcher Webster, and closely connected with him by marriage. He was naturally, therefore, often at Marshfield, and remained through life much in the Webster circle, — a position peculiarly agreeable to one of his genial temperament. He was the more fitted for it, because he sympathized strongly in that love of field sports which pervaded the atmosphere of Green Harbor. He was a good shot and an expert angler, so that he could offer congenial companionship even to the great statesman himself.

In the spring of 1858, and again in the autumn of 1859, he visited Europe with his wife and son.

Mrs. Joy died at their summer residence in Lynn, Mass., May 8, 1861. Her husband survived her just three years, and died at Marshfield, May 5, 1864.

HORACE KEATING.

HORACE KEATING was with the class in the freshman and sophomore years, and then left Cambridge. He afterwards went South, and became a planter in Mississippi, where he married a widow, and died in 1853 or 1854.

Of the striplings that went up to be examined the day after Commencement, 1829, none was brighter or handsomer than Horace Keating; but the above shadowy record gives all that can now be learned of him, even in the city of his birth, in whose immediate vicinity a large family connection continue to reside.

RUFUS TILDEN KING.

THE name of Rufus Tilden King appears on the annual catalogue of the first three years. He then left college, subsequently joined the class of 1834, and graduated with it.

RUFUS BIGELOW LAWRENCE.

THE name of Rufus Bigelow Lawrence appears on the annual catalogue of the first two years. He then left college, subsequently joined the class of 1834, and graduated with it.

WILLIAM HENRY MOODY.

WILLIAM HENRY MOODY, son of Paul and Susan L. Moody, was born in Byfield, Mass. His father was a distinguished mechanic, — one of those remarkable men whom the Lowells, the Jacksons, and the Bootts had the gift to draw around them in that busy decade following 1820, which ushered in the American factory system. The son came to college from Lowell, but his name appears on the annual catalogue only in the freshman year. At the end of it he left Cambridge and entered upon business pursuits. He married Martha, daughter of Dr. John Brickett, of Newburyport, and died at that place, November 7, 1841, leaving a widow and three daughters.

JOHN MURDOCH.

JOHN MURDOCH, after leaving college in the sophomore year, entered a counting-room in Boston. He left this for a similar position at New Orleans, where he remained several years.

In 1850 he returned to Boston, married Elizabeth, daughter of Mr. William Smith, a sea-captain of that port, and then went a second time to New Orleans. From that city he removed to St. Louis. Then he lived for many years in New York, where he was attached to the water-works. Finally he was employed in San Francisco.

In each place his longings to become an artist, and his occasional trials as such, prevented his entire success as a clerk. With early instruction in the profession that he loved, he would probably have attained distinction.

At San Francisco, he was struck down by paralysis. He was removed to the East, and died, May 16, 1871, at country lodgings in Pepperell, Mass.

His wife died several years before him. They had one son and four daughters. His son John (H. C. 1873) is now at Point Barrow, in Alaska, enlisted in the United States service as Observer, and in that of the Smithsonian Institute as Naturalist. His papers, published in the Boston Daily Advertiser, October 21 and November 4, 1882, give an interesting account of scientific life in the Arctic region.

Mr. Murdoch's daughters live with their relatives at Roxbury, Mass.

FRANCIS EBEN OLIVER.

FRANCIS EBEN OLIVER, son of Francis Johonnot and Mary Caroline (Alsop) Oliver, was born November 24, 1813. His father (H. C. 1795), who died in 1858, was a well-known and much respected citizen of Boston.

Our classmate's name appears in the annual catalogue only in the junior year. He was an invalid from childhood, and while a boy accompanied Mr. and Mrs. B. A. Gould to Europe, whence he returned in 1830. He entered college the following year, but was obliged to leave before becoming senior, on account of weakness of eyes. This and a great tendency to rheumatic affections prevented him from entering on any profession, and made him an exile. He travelled extensively, preferring the South of Europe and the vicinity of the Mediterranean, on which he was fond of cruising about in sailing vessels. He was in France and Italy on several occasions of great political excitement, and has left very complete journals filled with interesting details. He crossed the Atlantic many times, but the state of his health gradually curtailed the length of his Boston visits. The last three years of his life were passed abroad, and he died in London, June 9, 1850, at the age of thirty-seven. His remains were brought home and interred in the family tomb under King's Chapel.

Such is the short record of a man who was greatly loved and valued by the best of his contemporaries. Though largely cut off, by ill health, from facilities of acquiring knowledge, he yet became a well-read man generally, and a good belles-lettres scholar. He was a cultivated lover of art, and an extremely agreeable talker. It was his character, however, more than his accomplishments, that endeared him to his friends, — a genial, sunny nature, a spontaneous flow of spirits, triumphing over bodily ailments, made him a delightful companion, whose presence always brought cheer to a large home circle. But the epithet that best befits him is

"The grand old name of gentleman."

With that high ideal he must ever be associated, and it is recalled with the memory of his marked personal appearance, — his tall, slender figure, his refined expression, and his pale, dark skin, indicative of Huguenot descent.

LUCIUS PARKER.

THE name of Lucius Parker appears on the annual catalogue only in the freshman year. He then left college, subsequently joined the class of 1834, and graduated with it.

ISAAC CLARK PRAY.

TO those of the class who remember the freshman year, this name will recall an alert young man, prominent in class gatherings, and rather premature in all things, who had already the reputation of an author. It was a joke of Watson's that the society of the I. O. H. — born of our freshman year — "had a library chiefly consisting of Pray's works."

He left college at the end of the first year, and was lost sight of. Nearly forty years after, Jeffries Wyman, whose loyal heart kept all the traditions of our undergraduate days, says, in a letter dated July 4, 1868: "I went to Portland a few days since, when a youngish-looking gentleman put his hand on my shoulder, who proved to be nobody else than *the* poet of our class (not the class poet), on his way to make arrangements for a performance of the Bateman Opera Troupe. It was refreshing to learn how large a part he plays in the world, in writing for newspapers, in various services in the cause of the legitimate drama, translating operas into blank verse, aiding indigent individuals to opportunities for usefulness in connection with the press, and ever so much besides. He is the best preserved man of our whole number, and will compete even with Lowell."

It was not until it became necessary to learn something about him for Commencement, 1883, that the secretary found this sometime classmate had quite surpassed his early promise. In Drake's Dictionary of American Biography appears the following: "*Pray, Isaac Clark*, editor, author, and dramatist, born in Boston, 1813, died in New York, November 28, 1869. Graduated at Amherst College, 1833. Son of a Boston merchant of same name. Some time connected with the Journal of Commerce, and afterward wrote for the Herald; was the author of 'Virginius,' and was very successful as a theatrical manager. He trained many celebrities for the stage, among whom was Charlotte Cushman. He was in England in 1846-47, and performed successfully at the Queen's Theatre, London, and the Theatre Royal, Liverpool, and Cork, in the highest walk of the drama. Author of 'Prose and Verse,' 12mo, 1835; 'Poems,' 12mo, 1837; 'Book of the Drama,' 8vo, 1851; 'Memoirs of J. G. Bennett,' 1855; and of several burlesques and plays. Edited 'The Shrine,' a monthly, published at Amherst, 1831-33; 'Boston Pearl,' weekly, 1834; also many other magazines and reviews."

Dr. Charles Deane, of Cambridge, who kindly discovered the above, writes that Mr. Pray married Miss Helen Henry, of South Hadley, Mass., and had two children, daughters, now married.

OLIVER PRESCOTT.

OLIVER PRESCOTT, born in Boston, May 29, 1814, was the son of Samuel Jackson and Margaret (Hiller) Prescott. He entered Harvard College at the commencement of 1829, and remained during the freshman year, long enough to show his earnestness as a student; but before the next year began, he was obliged to leave on account of his eyes.

In April, 1831, he went to Cuba for the benefit of his health. He remained there a year, and returned much improved. He then took a situation in the Woodward High School at Cincinnati, to teach Latin and Greek. He next began the study of the law with Judge Timothy Walker of that city (H. C. 1826). He gave up this profession to become Pastor of the Swedenborgian Church in Cincinnati, in which office he remained till 1847.

He then returned to Boston and sailed for Europe, where he travelled one year. In 1848 he took charge of the Swedenborgian Society in Glasgow, Scotland. Here he married, June 5, 1849, Jessie Mackie, who died childless in 1854. In this year he took the name of Hiller, after his maternal grandfather, Major Joseph Hiller, a soldier of the Revolution, appointed by Washington the first Collector of Salem, Mass., then an important position. What rendered this change of name more attractive to our classmate was doubtless that Major Hiller was an early admirer of the writings of Baron Swedenborg, and imported the first entire set of his works that came to America.

Oliver Prescott Hiller went to London soon after his wife's death, took charge of the church there, and in 1864 married Emma Stokes.

He was all his life a hard student, in spite of defective vision. He is said to have spoken eloquently and to have reasoned closely, and though eccentric and somewhat hot-tempered he was honored wherever known, — a reputation easily credited by those who remembered him as a boy. His last literary work was a translation of the Psalms, left incomplete at his death. His last illness was from softening of the brain, brought on, it was thought, by overwork, his labor ceasing only with his life.

He died in London, May 11, 1870, leaving his widow and three children in that city, where they still reside.

WILLIAM SHIMMIN.

WILLIAM SHIMMIN was the son of William and Eliza (Parker) Shimmin, of Boston. He entered Harvard College at the Commencement of 1829, and left at the end of the freshman year.

On leaving college he went into a counting-room, and subsequently was in business in Boston and New York.

He married twice, and had five children, two sons and three daughters. The sons died before him. He himself died at St. Louis, Missouri, July 23, 1876.

HENRY WARING LATANE TEMPLE.

MR. TEMPLE was in the class during the freshman year only. To the secretary's inquiry of the postmaster at the place of his residence twenty-five years ago, the following answer came.

MILLER'S TAVERN, ESSEX CO., VA.,
October 23, 1882.

MR. WALDO HIGGINSON: —

Dear Sir, — I have been requested to answer your letter of inquiry about Rev. H. W. L. Temple. I am sorry to state that Mr. Temple died eleven years ago, February, 1871. He was for twenty years the faithful pastor of South Farnham Parish (P. E. C.) of Essex. Six children are now alive, — three sons and three daughters. The three sons are two in Arkansas and one in Texas. The three daughters live here in Essex. I married the oldest daughter, and will gladly furnish any additional information, if desired.

Yours truly,
WARNER LEWIS, M. D.

www.ingramcontent.com/pod-product-compliance
Lightning Source LLC
Chambersburg PA
CBHW030257170426
43202CB00009B/774